The
Girl
from
Dream
City

ALSO BY LINDA LEITH

FICTION
Birds of Passage (1993)
The Tragedy Queen (1995)
The Desert Lake (2006)

LITERARY NON-FICTION
*Introducing Hugh MacLennan's
Two Solitudes* (1990)
Marrying Hungary (2008)
Writing in the Time of Nationalism (2010)

ANTHOLOGY
*Telling Differences: New English
Fiction from Quebec* (1988)

TRANSLATION
Travels with an Umbrella: An Irish Journey,
translation into English of *Voyage en Irlande
avec un parapluie*, by Louis Gauthier (2004)

ESSAY
"Montreal in Wartime," introduction to Mavis
Gallant's play *What Is To Be Done?* (2017)

The Girl from Dream City

A LITERARY LIFE

Linda Leith

Printed and bound in Canada at Imprimerie Gauvin. The text of this book is printed on 100% post-consumer recycled paper with earth-friendly vegetable-based inks.

COVER AND TEXT DESIGN: Duncan Noel Campbell
COPY EDITOR: Kendra Ward
PROOFREADER: Caley Clements
COVER ART: "Paris, France" by Pierre Châtel-Innocenti / Unsplash.

Library and Archives Canada Cataloguing in Publication

TITLE: The girl from Dream City : a literary life / Linda Leith.

NAMES: Leith, Linda, author.

SERIES: Regina collection.

DESCRIPTION: Series statement: The Regina collection

IDENTIFIERS: Canadiana (print) 20200367501 | Canadiana (ebook) 20200368052 | ISBN 9780889777859 (softcover) | ISBN 9780889777873 (PDF) | ISBN 9780889777897 (EPUB)

SUBJECTS: LCSH: Leith, Linda. | CSH: Authors, Canadian (English)— 20th century—Biography. | LCSH: Montréal (Québec)—Biography. | LCSH: Montréal (Québec)—Intellectual life.| LCGFT: Autobiographies.

CLASSIFICATION: LCC PS8573.E49 Z46 2021 | DDC C813/.54—dc23

University of Regina Press

University of Regina, Regina, Saskatchewan, Canada, S4S 0A2
TEL: (306) 585-4758 FAX: (306) 585-4699
WEB: www.uofrpress.ca

10 9 8 7 6 5 4 3 2 1

We acknowledge the support of the Canada Council for the Arts for our publishing program. We acknowledge the financial support of the Government of Canada. / Nous reconnaissons l'appui financier du gouvernement du Canada. This publication was made possible with support from Creative Saskatchewan's Book Publishing Production Grant Program.

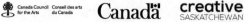

*For Nan and Desmond,
and Granny Jo,
with love.*

Contents

1.
Half-Told and Half-Forgotten

Whatever you say, say nothing.
—SEAMUS HEANEY, *North*

The Country Doctor

"When did Daddy propose to you?" I asked my mother, when I was old enough to wonder.

She hesitated. "I don't think he ever did," she said finally. She didn't refuse to answer; she simply said as little as possible. "We just knew."

I couldn't leave it at that. "Knew what?"

"We just knew we would get married."

Not a word more. She was such a private woman.

I wasn't satisfied. I'd wanted a story about a declaration. A ring, anyway. It was impossible to picture my father on bended knee.

I'm older now, and wiser, and I know romance when I see it. Sparing with words as my mother was, those were good words.

SHE HAD BEEN born in 1922, the year the Irish Free State came into being. Her parents had named her Annie

May, after the Chinese-American movie star Anna May Wong, but she always insisted on being called Nan.

Her own mother had, as it happened, also chosen her own name, Jo—in her case inspired by Jo March in *Little Women*. So, this was one thing my mother and grandmother had in common.

They were both bookish, too. When Nan was ill with a pulmonary disorder as a child, she took advantage of months of enforced idleness to read her way through the novels of Charles Dickens, which her mother borrowed on her weekly visits to the Linen Hall Library. On her return to school, she was an outstanding student, especially good at mathematics, and in her final year at Methodist College Belfast, she was offered a place at Trinity College Dublin.

Not having the means to send her to Trinity, her father appealed to his own father, who was well-to-do. He refused to help. The Ulster population, like the Scottish, valued education, but most of the time that meant education for men. There was no point in educating a woman, the argument went; a woman would get married and have children.

It was the great disappointment of Nan's life that she never got to university. She stayed in Belfast, became a teacher, and met Desmond Leith, who was a medical student at Queen's University.

Desmond's parents had been no more able than Nan's to send him to university, his own father having been a carpenter in the Belfast shipyards. But Desmond, too, had rich relatives—his mother's entrepreneurial brothers—and they were happy to cover the cost of sending him to "Inst," the Royal Belfast Academical Institution, and then to Queen's.

NAN AND DESMOND were like a Hollywood couple. Scarcely five feet tall, Nan was a glamorous redhead with clear blue eyes and high cheekbones, the very image of femininity. Desmond was brilliant, ambitious, and dashing. A missing front tooth, knocked out during a school cricket match, lent him an air of danger, like a buccaneer.

Desmond qualified in 1947, winning the university prize in gynecology, obstetrics, and surgery. Nan resigned her teaching position; they were married that summer and moved to the linen town of Lisburn, where my father spent five years as a country doctor. They had their first child, my brother Ian, the following spring, and I was born in late 1949.

Most patients saw Daddy in the surgery, but he made house calls, too. The telephone rang, and he picked up his heavy black bag and headed off at all hours to deliver a baby or tend to an ailing patient. Farm families who were short of cash stopped by the house with fresh produce, which was as precious as rubies in those days of postwar rationing. Some of them continued to show their appreciation to the young doctor even after the National Health Service came in.

SO, OUR KITCHEN table was laden with churned butter and eggs. "We'll have cake for our tea," Mummy said, pulling her apron over her head and tying it behind her.

She turned on the oven and took sugar and flour down from the shelf. She prepared the cake tin with the butter wrapper and a dusting of flour, then pulled out the crockery bowl from under the counter, a wooden spoon from the drawer, and a measuring cup from the cupboard.

She'd learned how to bake from scrupulous Methodist teachers. Ian stood with his fingers on the edge of the counter, watching her every move. I sat in the high chair, mesmerized.

Nan held the big bowl in the crook of her arm and creamed the butter with sugar before cracking the eggs into the mix and stirring until it was all gloopy. She measured the flour and sifted it with baking soda and a pinch of salt, folded the dry ingredients into the wet, then tipped the contents of the bowl into the tin and popped it in the oven.

Ian got to lick the spoon, and I scraped the bowl.

THE SOUNDTRACK OF our days was dominated by politics. It was in 1948 that the Labour government brought in the National Health Service, and there was never a time that I didn't hear about that. So, I knew more than most little girls about NHS coverage of vision care, which was cut when it proved too costly.

"There *was* a tremendous demand for glasses," Daddy acknowledged. We were in the kitchen, and he had a drink in front of him, probably Scotch and water, just a drop of water; more than enough water went into the making of whisky, and there was no call to add more than another drop.

Mummy sipped her gin and tonic, her legs crossed.

"Hundreds of thousands of patients," Daddy went on, "went to doctors' surgeries all over the country looking for glasses the very minute the NHS came into being."

His voice rose. "And people *complain* about that! Holy Mary, Mother of God! As though it's a scandal for people to benefit from the NHS!"

He paused for effect; he had a comic's sense of timing. Mummy said nothing. It wasn't that she'd heard this argument from Desmond before, although she had. She was waiting for the punchline.

Ian and I waited, too. I was enthralled, but also on edge; Desmond always had that effect on me. He was not a tall man, though I thought him a giant, but he was a compelling speaker, even when his audience consisted only of Mummy, Ian, and me. Compelling and alarming. It might be that he was most compelling with just this audience of three.

"But that is not the scandal," he said, modulating his voice. "The scandal is that every blessed one of those patients had been doing without glasses their whole lives. These are people of all ages—men and women in their sixties and seventies and eighties—and they'd never before been able to afford a pair of glasses."

His voice rose again. He might have been preparing to stand up in the House of Commons to make a speech. "The scandal is that those men and women had never been able to bloody *see*!"

IN 1951, NAN and Desmond went on a road trip across France and into Italy with their friends, John Stewart, a BBC journalist, and his wife, Joan, who was a foodie before there were foodies. Enjoying foods and wines undreamed of in the long years of rationing and austerity, they came home with new resolve. Determined to find ways to make some of the dishes she had eaten on the continent, Joan started feeding Irish snails a steady diet of parsley as a prelude to making *escargots à la bourguignonne*. Nan and Desmond decided to leave

Northern Ireland for good. It would take them a year to find the way out.

I WAS NOT yet three when we packed our bags for London. Everyone on board the Liverpool boat was out on deck as the big engines churned and Northern Ireland moved into the past. Stalwart Ulster men and women were singing and swaying.

Mummy and Daddy exchanged looks. They had a secret language, those two, and could communicate without saying a word. I listened. Maybe the words of the song would give me a clue about what my parents were thinking. I heard, "I love to wear the sash my father wore."

Daddy didn't like this, for some reason, and muttered something to Nan about "muscular Christians," then led us all below deck to the bar.

"What's wrong, Mummy?" I asked.

"They shouldn't be singing sectarian songs," she said. She was pregnant, moving carefully as we picked our way down the steep metal stairs. "Orange songs."

"Orange songs?" How could a song be orange?

"Songs that are for one group only," she said. "Divisive songs."

I still didn't understand.

Haddon Hall

Haddon Hall was a sprawling mansion set well back from Southend Road in the London borough of Beckenham. With a circular driveway, a vast garden, and a magnificent staircase, it had been built in Victorian times for a local dignitary, but had been converted into apartments by the time we moved into the ground floor flat. It became increasingly dilapidated after we left, four years later, and its last hurrah was as the birthplace of Ziggy Stardust in the late '60s, when David Bowie was living there. Haddon Hall was demolished in the 1980s and replaced by the apartment buildings that stand there now.

Daddy walked the short distance to Beckenham Junction every morning to take the train into central London. He and Nan were now members of the Communist Party of Great Britain, and he was the editor of *Medical World*, a magazine run by a collective of communist doctors in North London.

My brothers and I—Brian was born soon after we moved in—were surrounded by books, long before we could read. By the books that had crossed the Irish Sea with us, certainly, but by far more than the ones on our bookshelves. By the books Nan and Desmond had left behind in Northern Ireland, as well, and by those Granny Jo had taken out of the Linen Hall Library in Belfast every week—more books than I can ever name.

Beckenham was busy in a way that Lisburn had never been busy, and we walked to the high street every day—Brian in the pram, Ian and I holding onto the handles—so we got to know all these new shops and shopkeepers. We learned we had to look left, then right, then left again before we crossed the road. Ian was four, old enough to start reading. Mummy took us into the local bookshop to buy *Dick and Jane*, and soon taught us both to read.

In the afternoon, she put on the radio for *Listen with Mother*. She made us a simple tea of boiled eggs or baked beans on toast and started chopping onions and garlic for the enticing dinner she and Desmond would eat when we were all in bed. They went to the cinema to see Marlon Brando in *A Streetcar Named Desire* or Cary Grant and Marilyn Monroe in *Monkey Business*. They went to party meetings, and on weekends we all joined in demonstrations and Ban the Bomb marches.

MY GRANDPARENTS CAME over from Belfast, and I rejoiced. I knew them well and adored Granny Jo especially. She and I settled into a comfortable chair together, sitting quietly for the longest times. She told me stories and sang songs. One of the songs was about a young Irishman digging for gold in the streets of London—except that, "For all that I found there, I might as well be /

Where the Mountains of Mourne sweep down to the sea." I loved that.

She recited poems from her own childhood, too. One of her favourites, William Allingham's "The Fairies," became my favourite, as well:

> Up the airy mountain,
> Down the rushy glen,
> We daren't go a-hunting
> For fear of little men;
> Wee folk, good folk,
> Trooping all together;
> Green jacket, red cap,
> And white owl's feather![1]

I was intrigued. I'd heard about the wee folk, and I loved the rhythm of trooping up the mountain and down into the glen. "Airy" was a new word to me, as was "rushy," which made me think of streams rushing down from the mountain. The repetition of "folk" and the togetherness of these "wee folk, good folk" infuse the poem with a bright energy, as does their colourful apparel. The white owl's feather is perfect.

But this is a poem about fear, too, about not daring to go a-hunting, "For fear of little men." Chilling as well as intriguing, in other words, especially as I never could figure out who "we" are. Who is it, exactly, who doesn't dare go a-hunting? Not the wee folk, certainly. People like Granny Jo? Mummy and Daddy? Me?

I asked many times. Granny Jo was always happy to talk, so why was she so vague about the wee folk who had peopled her childhood on the Donegal coast? And the poet's childhood, too, for William Allingham had grown up on the other side of Donegal Bay.

I wanted her to reassure me that the wee folk were good folk. Wasn't that what the poem said? There was no such reassurance. The wee folk could be wicked. You had to beware of little men.

They weren't ogres, though; they were too small to be ogres. More like goblins? I couldn't picture them, and Granny Jo was of no help at all on what they looked like.

I was never frightened, listening to the poem. I loved its mystery, I loved Granny Jo's musical voice, I loved the scent of her face cream and powder, and I felt safe in her arms.

Mummy took us all with her to smelly old Euston Station to say goodbye when my grandparents went home to Belfast. Granny Jo cried on the platform, and I did, too.

THE *Medical World* offices were in Bloomsbury, and when Daddy got home from work, his stories were filled with meetings—editorial meetings, board meetings, meetings with journalists and printers, illustrators, designers, advertisers—and punctuated with pub lunches and drinks after work.

Faber & Faber had their offices nearby, on Great Russell Street, and Desmond spent time with editors and with some of the writers Faber & Faber was publishing in the early 1950s. One of the authors was the fine Belfast poet Louis MacNeice, whom my parents had known when he made return visits to Belfast, and who was now working for the BBC in London.

It was a far cry from the life of a country doctor in Lisburn.

As a small child, I had no sense of that. It was later, much later, that I started wondering if the excitement of being in London had gone to his head. Nan realized he was having an affair when he started staying in town after work. No one now knows what happened to the meals she had prepared for him on the evenings that he didn't get home until the wee hours, but that's when the rows began.

THEN, ONE AFTERNOON, a delegation of women, seven in all, appeared in front of Haddon Hall.

My brothers and I were in the kitchen with Mummy when she saw them making their way up the circular driveway. She lifted Brian out of his playpen and turned to Ian and me. "Come with me, please," she said. "I want you all in your room for a bit."

I started to close my book.

"Quick!" she added.

The doorbell rang, and she put Brian down in our bedroom and closed the door. I heard her steps across the hall; I heard murmurs, unfamiliar voices, and shuffling as she let them in.

Our flat was big, but not that big. The women raised their voices. I couldn't make out what they were saying, but I did hear Mummy's silence. Mummy was good at silence.

One woman's voice was louder than the others', and she raised it again. More silence, more hubbub, then more shuffling. I heard the front door close.

Mummy opened the bedroom door. "It's time for our tea," she said. Not one word more.

I WOULDN'T FIND out for more than forty years why those women came to see my mother. Daddy was long dead, Mummy was living alone in a sprawling old house in Canterbury, and I was staying with her for a week.

This was one of many visits I made to my mother in her old age. After our dinner, we talked about her parents, her childhood, the boyfriends she'd had before she met Desmond—filling in the gaps between what I remembered, what I knew, and what I had never been able to figure out.

One evening, we talked about Haddon Hall. One memory leading to another, we also talked about the Communist Party, and I was reminded of the women who came to the door that long-ago afternoon.

"Who *were* those women?" I asked. Seven women. It was like something out of a fairy tale.

She took a breath, and I could feel her considering how she would respond.

"I had fallen in love," she said finally.

This was a surprise. "Who with?"

She picked up her glass of vermouth and ginger ale and held it in both hands.

"I had fallen in love with a man called Stanley."

"Stanley?" I had never heard of Stanley.

She took a sip of her drink.

"Stanley was an electrician," she said after a bit. "And he was a party member, too. We had met at the meetings Desmond and I went to."

"And what happened?"

"Stanley and I fell in love." Her voice had slowed, ever so slightly.

I waited.

"His wife found out," she said.

"About you and Stanley."

"Yes. And one day, she came to see me at Haddon Hall."

"With her friends," I said.

She looked at me, nodded.

"And?"

"And that was the end of that."

SO, THAT'S HOW I learned about what happened when I was a little girl. Many of my earliest memories are inaccessible, and I was not a witness to all the drama of our years in Beckenham. Much of what I do know about that time comes from those evenings I spent with my mother in Canterbury.

The God That Failed

It was in 1954, when I was four, that the party sent Desmond to Bucharest on a fact-finding mission on medicine in communist Romania. He spent ten days there and came home with hand-painted bowls and vividly coloured woven goods, opening up a window on a foreign world. I remember touching the rough pottery of the dishes. They were like nothing I had ever known. I stroked the thick weave of the fabric. These were textures I had never felt, colours I had never seen.

He came home with something else, too: his professional opinion as a doctor. Far from being impressed, he had been appalled by medical practice in Romania. It was an assessment that would change his life, Nan's life, all our lives, forever.

Desmond had long since lost any belief in the God he had grown up with in his Belfast childhood, replacing faith in God with faith in a sunny socialist future. He had hoped, as his comrades in the party had hoped, that he would be inspired by the strides the Romanians had taken in health care. He was shocked to discover the wretched truth, however, and as a doctor who knew good medicine from bad, he knew that Romanian medicine was a disgrace.

He was aware that the party faithful in London would be shocked, too. His comrades were expecting a glowing report on medical care in Romania. That's why they had sent him there, to confirm their belief in the superiority of the communist system.

He went to the meeting and presented his damning report. Had he hoped he could convince his comrades he was right? He must have known that was wishful thinking. How could they believe him? It was impossible for them both to believe him and maintain their faith in communism.

And, indeed, one indignant Irish doctor was no match for the Communist Party of Great Britain. Desmond and Nan quit the party.

THIS WAS WRENCHING, for the party had been at the centre of their lives since the move to London.

There was worse to come.

Quitting the party made it impossible for Desmond to continue working with the collective of communist doctors at *Medical World,* so he also lost his job.

In a matter of days, Nan and Desmond had parted company not only with the utopian faith that had underpinned their lives but with almost everyone they had known in London. And now Desmond was out of work with a wife and three children to support.

IT WAS TOO much for him. He suffered an emotional breakdown and disappeared one day without a word. He was missing for two weeks, and Nan had no idea where he had gone.

Ian and I had no idea he'd gone missing, and Brian was not yet two.

Then, one day, we got home from the shops to find the kitchen in disarray, with dirty dishes in the sink, the frying pan on the stove, and an open packet of sausages on the counter. Someone had cooked a big breakfast while we were out. Nan went into the bedroom.

There was a stranger in the bed she shared with Desmond. A bearded vagrant, fast asleep, snoring.

Daddy had been in France, sleeping rough.

France! How he must have loved France, on that trip with the Stewarts—that had been only three years earlier, another era.

FROM BAD TO worse—and then far worse, for that was when Ian got sick.

It started with a fever, then a cough. Mummy looked after him at home at first, but days went by, and he became seriously ill. His fever was dangerously high and his cough painful when an ambulance pulled up to take him to hospital. Mummy climbed into the ambulance with him, and I stayed home to look after Brian.

I had lots of practice looking after Brian—there was no other babysitter, except when Granny Jo was around—but I wasn't used to being on my own, without Ian. The house seemed bigger than ever, especially in the dark.

There were other anxieties, too. I couldn't under-stand why Ian was sick. Mummy said little to me about that, and Daddy was volatile, angry, when he was home. They had terrible rows, night after night, and Daddy's shouting wakened me.

After weeks in the local hospital, Ian was sicker than ever, gravely ill with double pneumonia and whooping cough. Desmond ranted about the hospital, the doctors, the staff, then used his medical connections to move Ian to a different hospital. The new hospital was better, but it was farther away, too, so Nan was now gone much of the day. Brian and I were not allowed to go anywhere near Ian, for fear of infection.

AND THEN DADDY disappeared again, this time—as I eventually learned—because he had been hospitalized for treatment of manic depression.

How did Nan pay for groceries? How did she pay the rent? How did she see her future? She could have found work as a teacher again, but that wasn't going to pay the bills anytime soon. And there were bills to pay, some of them long overdue.

Did any of their former comrades help her out? Did she ever ask for help? Desmond had burned that bridge, and Nan's lover, Stanley, was no help at all. How could he be? His wife had put a stop to that.

The uncertainty must have been the worst of it. Did Nan dare visit the branch manager at Barclay's Bank, when she had no way of knowing how long it would be until Desmond would be employed again? She must have. Did she talk to anyone? How did she cope?

Nan and Desmond had been married for almost eight years. They had lost their social circle, Ian was in critical condition, and Desmond was unemployed and mentally ill.

They both had family in Belfast, but neither Desmond's parents nor Nan's could help them out financially. And no force on earth could have persuaded them to move back across the Irish Sea.

EVENTUALLY, IAN STARTED to get better. When he was almost well enough to come home, Mummy took Brian and me with her to visit him. Ian was thin and pale and serious, and his eyes looked bigger than they should. He was sitting up in a vast hospital bed in a threadbare hospital gown. He had puzzle books and comic books and a few small toys I had never seen.

Secrets

It took Ian a long time to regain his full strength, but at least he was now home. This meant Mummy was home a lot more as well, and looking after Brian. I started school, which was when I realized that Ian had missed what should have been his first year.

I discovered a cluster of small green plants growing in a corner of the garden. The only photograph I've seen of the garden comes from later on, after we'd left Haddon Hall. It shows David Bowie with long, straight hair, in a floral maxi-dress. You can't see the plants growing in the corner.

I didn't know what plant this was, with its pointed leaves, but I picked a leaf and smelled it. Not much smell. I studied it, deciding if I wanted to eat it. Mummy had taught us never to eat anything we happened to find outdoors, where berries and mushrooms could be poisonous.

So, I knew about the danger and I ate it anyway. I put the leaf on my tongue and nibbled it. It tasted fresh and slightly tart, like . . . what? Wild strawberries, perhaps. Or rosehip. I ate one leaf, then another.

I looked for this plant whenever I was outside—and when no one was looking. For this was a secret pleasure, always the best kind. I didn't tell Nan, for she would have put a stop to it, and I didn't want to stop.

When we moved again, in 1956, we moved to such a foreign world that I forgot I'd ever discovered a secret pleasure all my own.

I HAD BEEN miserable without Ian, but I hadn't missed Desmond, when he was away. He was such an overpowering man. I wasn't aware of any of the life-changing developments in his life, all our lives—not the ones that had just taken place, not the ones that were imminent. Nothing was said, nothing was explained. My parents were from Northern Ireland, after all, where secrecy is like mother's milk. No one was to know about their membership in the Communist Party, and no one was to know about Desmond's illness.

I was too young to understand, in any case. I knew nothing, sensed everything, and there didn't seem to be enough air to breathe properly, but I was only five years old; I didn't know how to put any of this into words. And Ian had missed out on so much that he had no way of knowing the secrets he and I were both supposed to keep.

And who would we have told? There was no one we could have talked to, even if we'd wanted to. Even if we'd known what to say.

I SPENT DECADES thinking about it. Even now, I sometimes waken with a question I would love to ask Nan.

How long was it until Daddy found work again? And how did he manage that? Would any of those communist doctors have given him a reference?

I always wished I could ask Desmond himself, but asking Desmond was dangerous. He could turn on you in an instant and demolish you before you even knew it. He had a Victorian attitude to children and was often impatient with us. I was less and less able please him as I grew older, no matter how hard I tried, and we had been estranged for years when he died suddenly in 1984.

THE TRIP ACROSS the Irish Sea turned out to have been the start of years of wandering from one country to another, and the family grew every time we moved to a new city. It was soon after we moved into Haddon Hall in 1952 that Brian was born. By the time Sheelagh came along, four years later, we were living in Basel. After three years in Switzerland, we returned to London in 1959, and Mandy was born in 1963, a few months before we boarded RMS *Carinthia* and sailed across the Atlantic to Montreal.

It was unusual for a professional family that was non-religious to have so many children, but this was what Nan and Desmond wanted. They must have known this would be their whole world. There was no other.

It was and is unusual, too, for a family to move as often as we did, and to move internationally. My father had started climbing the corporate ladder—a steep ascent until the early 1970s, when the family left Montreal for Brussels, and then a lurching descent after the move to Nairobi in 1972, then back to Brussels two years later, and the final move to Canterbury. The families of diplomats and families in the armed forces sometimes move more than we did, but they move within a context that provides structure and continuity. I have encountered few others who moved in isolation as much as we did.

By the time the *Carinthia* docked in Montreal on Nan's forty-first birthday, I was thirteen years old and had left so much behind with every move that I had forgotten not only a secret pleasure but also friends I had loved, schools, cities, entire countries, and languages I once spoke fluently.

THERE WERE TWO steadying influences in all these moves. One was family—a family of seven, when we boarded the *Carinthia*. Granny Jo made it eight, for she lived with us on and off for years after she was widowed.

The family was a world unto itself, always there when everything else was unrecognizable. It had limitations, though, as steadying influences go, for it was sometimes troubled, and fraught with anger.

Desmond had occasionally alarmed me in Lisburn. Inspiring and dazzling as he was, there was always something about him that was too much—too passionate, too ambitious, too intense, too marvellous, and always unreachable, unknowable, ineffable. I never felt entirely comfortable with him, ever.

What had been alarming in Lisburn darkened after the rupture with the Communist Party, which is when my parents' natural tendency to keep themselves to themselves turned from reticence to secrecy. This was air I breathed often, as I grew up, as colourless and odourless as carbon monoxide.

Something had happened, but what? I was aware as a child under ten is aware, with great certainty but none of the words I needed—no way of turning it into a story. Nothing, ever, was said.

There were only two people who knew the story, and neither one was telling. One was Desmond, who was more distant than ever, as unapproachable and frightening as the great Oz. It was as though he were curtained off from my brothers and me, except that the curtain was invisible, so there was no way of knowing where it was—or where he had gone.

Nan was the other person who knew the story, and she wasn't letting on, not back then. Not to Ian and me, certainly, not to Granny Jo, not to anyone at all. Desmond had been dead for twenty years by the time I discovered what was behind the secrecy that settled over us in Beckenham.

It was a good childhood for a writer. I learned to be observant, and to make up stories to explain the situation I was in—and the situations others were in, too. I learned to be wary, because I never really knew what was going on. And I learned to be patient, which was essential. Just look at how long it has taken me to piece it all together.

BOOKS WERE THE other steadying influence. By the time I could read for myself, books made sense to me in ways that nothing else made sense. Growing up without religion, as I did, writers seemed like divine beings.

This was a view that survived meeting some of the writers my parents knew. Alec, a historian who had taught Desmond at Inst, had a house up the Antrim coast, not far from the Giant's Causeway, and he roasted a chicken for us all when we paid him a summer visit.

The Bushmills distillery was within hailing distance of the house, and the whiskey had been flowing freely ever since we arrived. "Is that bird not done yet?" Alec asked, leaning on the table to help him get to his feet. "I could eat a horse."

He pulled out the roasting pan and stuck a fork in the chicken. "Done!" he announced. "Time to eat!"

He found a knife in the drawer and set about carving the chicken.

Daddy watched him, then flashed Mummy a look before pulling plates down from the cupboard and setting the kitchen table for three. What was this secret language they used? I saw that look, and it meant nothing to me, but Mummy nodded. She got it.

"Here you go!" Alec said, plunking one plate in front of Ian—my brothers and I had been seated in the lounge—and another in front of me, before heading back to the kitchen.

Nan set a third plate down for Brian. "The vegetables are all right," she said in a low voice, "but don't eat the chicken. It isn't cooked properly."

So that was it. Daddy had been alerting Mummy about the chicken. Which might have made me doubt Alec's divinity, but he was a writer, and nothing could make me doubt his divinity. I did doubt his practicality, but then divine creatures have little need of practical skills.

NO WRITER I read in my youth could help me understand the worlds in which I grew up, but books did open up worlds that made sense. Not thin, realistic stories about girls in school uniform and boys with their hair parted. Those interested me well enough, like anthropological research on a remote population, but what I really wanted were other kinds of stories altogether, stories as rich and colourful—and alarming—as the life I knew, with wee folk, goblins, dwarves, and ogres. The taller these tales were, the more plausible I found them.

I read hungrily, hoping to find a sentence or two that applied to me. There were few such sentences, and that's what kept me reading. There had to be someone who knew, someone who had written what I needed to read.

That's why I myself had to become a writer.[2] And it was writing that eventually allowed me to excavate some of what had been tucked away in the hidden recesses of my mind, like a language learned in childhood and soon forgotten.

MY MOTHER SURVIVED in the house in Canterbury until New Year's Eve, 2011, but now she's gone, too. We became closer in the last decades of her life than we had been since we crossed the Atlantic to Montreal. I asked her why she had not protected me from my father's rage when I was growing up, and the question surprised her, for I had never challenged her before. She dealt with this well, and we moved on to the best conversations we ever had.

She was extraordinarily healthy, and her memory was sharp. She was as coquettish as she had been as a young woman, with a lover who had come into her antique shop and—she was eighty by this time—told her she was the most beautiful woman he had ever seen. Her high cheekbones were more pronounced than ever, and her hair was long and grey.

Her eyesight was poor, though, and her knees were weak, so she rarely left the house, fearing she might fall on the cobblestoned streets. She didn't want Pam, her Kentish cleaning woman, to clean indoors, lest she move anything. Pam didn't mind; she adored Nan, whom she saw as a goddess of cosmopolitan sophistication, which was about right. Nan did allow her to polish the door knocker, and a knocker never gleamed more brightly than the brass lion on the front door of 52 Stour Street. Pam spent the rest of the morning picking up items Nan needed at the local health food store or at Debenham's on the high street, when she needed a new lipstick or moisturizer from the Elizabeth Arden counter.

It was finally possible for Mummy and me to talk about everything we had never been able to talk about— about Stanley, about the women at the door of Haddon Hall, about the times Daddy had disappeared. And that was when she finally told me the most closely guarded secret of all.

"After he got back from France," she said, "he saw an eminent Spanish psychiatrist who was practising in London. He diagnosed Desmond with manic depression. They call it bipolar disorder nowadays. He was admitted to hospital and treated with electric shock therapy. And that was terrible, so terrible that he refused it when he needed treatment again, later on."

Had I ever known he had been diagnosed as bipolar? I searched my memory and came up blank. I hadn't known when I was a child, and I hadn't known later, either.

"By that time, they had given the treatment a different name," she said. "Electroconvulsive therapy. But it was the same thing."

"When was that?" I asked.

"Oh, much later." She pondered for a minute. "It must have been twenty years later. Early 1970s. The psychiatrist Desmond saw at that point tried to reassure him that this electroconvulsive therapy was much better than the shock treatment they'd used in the 1950s."

Some of this I had been aware of, for I'd been a student when Daddy was hospitalized in London in the early 1970s. I had never known about the electroconvulsive therapy, though, and I had never known he'd been hospitalized with bipolar disorder.

My parents had been living in Nairobi in 1971, when Mummy phoned me to let me know that Daddy had had what she called a "breakdown." A year or so later, when I was a student in London, she called me again, after he'd suffered a more serious breakdown.

"So, Daddy refused electroconvulsive therapy, that second time?" I asked her after dinner in her kitchen in Canterbury.

"He wanted nothing to do with it. He'd found it brutal."

Poor Daddy.

I HAD KNOWN other bits of what she told me on those evenings, but so much of this story was new.

Mummy loved Daddy, and he adored her; none of that was ever in doubt, but my own feelings about my father had always been complicated.

By the time my mother told me these stories, she had been a widow for years, and I had had time to do a lot of thinking about the father I had always found so difficult.

I had learned more about the idealism my parents shared as a young couple facing a future together at the end of the war. About Daddy's admiration for two towering figures, both doctors—the fiction writer A.J. Cronin, and Aneurin Bevan, minister of health in the postwar Labour government—who had revolutionized the practice of medicine in the UK.

I had seen for myself how sweetly, and with what concern, Daddy wrote to his parents in their old age. That was a side of him I had rarely seen, and I wished I had known him better.

By this time, I myself had been back to Northern Ireland, too, where I'd been surprised to meet a Lisburn woman of about my age who told me that my father had brought her into the world. I'd been stunned to learn that he'd been considered a very gentle doctor.

Gentle? My father?

SO, I WAS ready to hear more, dying to hear more. And that's how it happened that, evening after evening, on successive visits to Canterbury, my mother told me stories I had never heard before, and she and I were able to share poignant memories of my father.

I had become a writer, by this time, and I started taking notes as my mother spoke. She was pleased about that. She wanted a record of her adventures, and I was the most likely person to write about them. "I've had *such* an interesting life," she told me more than once. "It would be a pity if no one knew."

2.
The
Golden
Years

There is always one moment
in childhood when the door
opens and lets the future in.
—GRAHAM GREENE,
The Power and the Glory

Mirror Calm

My parents pieced their marriage back together, and Desmond did an about-turn and reinvented himself as medical director of Sandoz, a multinational pharmaceutical company based in Basel.

How did he manage that? His membership in the Communist Party must have been an obstacle. Even if his mental illness had been kept quiet, it must have been known that he'd been out of work.

Someone must have put a good word in for him. A corporate advertiser? Someone from Sandoz, which would have had a London office? The pharmaceutical companies did advertise in *Medical World*.

It was the summer of 1956 when Desmond whisked us all away from the smog of London to the clear blue skies of Switzerland.

WE SPENT THREE years in Basel, but this was such a radical move into another world that I forgot all about that time as soon as we returned to London. I forgot the languages I had learned in Switzerland. I forgot the school I walked to, Sevogel Schule. I forgot all about Madeleine Tripet, who was my first friend. Those years simply vanished.

If someone mentioned Basel to me, yes, I would nod at the reminder. When I had to account for my schooling on a resumé or an application form, yes, I did include Seevogel Schule, 1956 to 1959, having forgotten the right spelling of "Sevogel." But nothing about Basel came to mind without a direct prompt.

Why was that? And how could that happen? How could I forget three years of my life?

MORE THAN THIRTY years after we left Basel, a magazine editor in Montreal asked me to write a short piece about books that had had an impact on me as a girl. That was when I remembered the books I'd had in Basel.

I jotted down a few notes, and in the process of writing, I did now remember the books—and more. It was in working on that magazine piece that I rediscovered Basel in an eternal present untouched by everything that went before and everything that came after.

IT'S THE BEGINNING of September. Mummy and I are making our way from our apartment on St-Alban-Anlage to Sevogel Schule. Brian will soon be four years old, and Mummy is holding his hand. She is expecting another baby.

With us are a neighbour, Frau Tripet, and her daughter Madeleine, who speak a language I haven't heard before. They are French-speaking, from Geneva, but Frau Tripet is able to communicate with Mummy in English. Our apartment building has different entrances, and the Tripet family lives in the section next to ours. Madeleine and I are in the same class.

I don't remember learning German, perhaps because I pick it up so quickly. In class, we learn Hochdeutsch, standard German, and in the playground we speak the local dialect, Baslerdütsch. My family name is pronounced in the German way, so I have become Linda Light.

Ian is eight years old. Having missed so much school when he was ill, he takes the streetcar across Basel to a school where he is taught in English. Brian is going to *Kindergarten* and has learned Baslerdütsch overnight.

Madeleine and I dress up as nurses after school on a September afternoon. Where did we get the cap and apron emblazoned with a red cross? It's unlikely Mummy would have found one such outfit for me, even less likely she'd have thought to get one for Madeleine, as well. Did Frau Tripet make them? Nan would never go to such lengths; she wasn't that kind of mother—she never sewed anything; she had dressmakers—and the idea would never have occurred to her.

Madeleine and I feel very important as we parade up and down St-Alban-Anlage waiting for the taxi to arrive. Passersby smile at us indulgently, and a few stop to chat.

"Are you waiting for someone?" one woman asks.

"*Ja*," I say.

"We're waiting for Linda's baby sister to arrive," Madeleine explains. "She's just been born!"

"Mummy and Daddy are bringing her back from the hospital any minute," I add.

"What is her name?"

Madeleine looks at me; she's not sure.

"Her name is Sheelagh Maya," I say.

The woman hesitates, then says, "Maya is such a pretty name."

Sheelagh is not a name she is familiar with, but she knows Maya.

"And you're going to look after her?"

We answer in unison. "*Ja!*"

The taxi arrives. The baby, who is born on Brian's fourth birthday, is swaddled in white broderie anglaise. She has just a little hair, very fine, the palest strawberry blonde. She's beautiful.

THERE IS SUNSHINE, in this new life, and there are no rows. I walk to school with Madeleine, and we play together after we get home. I feed and change Sheelagh. I iron handkerchiefs and tea towels. I read *Eagle* and *Bunty*, the comics magazines that Granny Jo posts to Ian and me from Belfast every week. When the good weather comes, I walk to the Sankt-Jakob swimming pool and learn to swim. These years in Basel are a golden time.

Mummy, now Frau Doktor Light, manages to make the extraordinary seem ordinary enough. The city is immaculate, the Rhine stately. Nan loves the shop windows, where chocolates and *Basler Leckerli* and lingerie are like gifts from the gods. She buys fresh fruit and vegetables from a cart driven by a man who keeps himself cool by hanging grapes over his ears. She makes *Bircher Müesli* for breakfast, grating apple and hazelnuts and lemon zest over raw oats, then topping it off with yogurt.

When Mummy doesn't understand what people say, which is practically all the time, she enlists my help. I run downstairs every day to the Konsum, the convenience store on the ground floor of our building. Mummy tries enlisting Brian's help, too, but he rattles away at her in Baslerdütsch, unaware that she can't follow what he is saying.

Herr Doktor Light doesn't speak any more German than his Frau, but the people he works with speak English. He is steadier than I have known him—than I will ever know him. I still find him intimidating, and I seldom speak to him unless he has asked me a question, but I am less anxious than I was in Beckenham.

My brothers and I have had our tea by the time Desmond gets home from work. He takes off his jacket and tie, pours himself a drink, and listens to the BBC World Service news about Suez and the Hungarian Revolution. Hungary is a lot closer to home than Suez, and there are fears the Russian tanks rolling into Budapest may not stop at the Austrian border. Baslers have started to hoard food, and refugees are fleeing across Austria into Switzerland, so that the Red Cross has set up a refugee centre in Basel.

The Hungarian Revolution is closer to home emotionally, too, for my parents have their own experience of standing up to communist authority. It has some emotional impact on me, too, for I am absorbing almost everything from my parents. That now includes the intensity of their interest in the news about Hungary. Nan takes my brothers and Sheelagh and me to the refugee centre to donate some clothing and toys, including a teddy bear of mine.

Is this the reason I will grow up to marry a Hungarian refugee? No. The question is almost too ridiculous to ask. I'm only six years old, for a start. And I really don't care about that teddy bear, which is no great loss.

But the ferment around the 1956 revolution does alert me to the existence of Hungary and Hungarians, and to some slight awareness of their history. Might that predispose me, at least, to taking an interest in the debonair Hungarian I meet when I'm eighteen?

DADDY TRAVELS TO London on business and brings books back with him. Some are for Nan and himself, and others are for Ian and me. There is no English bookshop in Basel, and my parents want us to have books to read. I get *Heidi,* which I enjoy, and *The Swiss Family Robinson,* which I thought might cast some light on the Swiss family Leith. It does nothing of the kind.

The book I love best is a big, lavishly illustrated book about Native Americans. Where does this come from? Not from a London bookshop, certainly; this is not a book Daddy would ever choose. It's not a book to read, really, more a coffee-table book. Do we pick it up at the refugee centre? Surely not. The point there is to donate goods the refugees needed, not to come home with treasure. Or is it a present from some visiting American? I suppose that's a possibility, though it seems to appear out of nowhere.

This book sweeps me off my feet. I don't read it in the hope of discovering anything about my own experience, anything useful at all. This is pure fantasy, an imagined world unlike anything I have ever known, anything I will ever know, utterly foreign. Thinking about it today—I have no way of tracing the book—I figure it must have been a fantasy to the author, too, who likely had about as much Indigenous heritage as I did.

The cover is as lush and creamy as gelato, and the illustrations idealize a culture I would like to believe in. The print is large, the pages are heavy, as though each one carries more weight than it can bear. One section outlines the materials and techniques needed to make a

2. The Golden Years

Native American headdress. There are line drawings of every step and entire pages with full-colour illustrations of magnificent finished headdresses.

It doesn't look easy, exactly, but I'm a capable girl. I could do it. This book would be my guide. All I need are the right materials.

But where can I find feathers, beads, strips of leather, and the tools I need?

It's hopeless, I know. I won't ever find what's needed—not as a little Irish girl in Basel, of all places. Not anywhere, ever.

MY BROTHERS AND I share a bedroom, and for weeks after Daddy gets back from London, he reads *Treasure Island* to us once we're all tucked in. This is one of the books he brought back for Ian. Desmond enjoyed it when he himself was a lad, and he wants us to enjoy it, too.

He reads splendidly, pacing the narration, putting on different accents for each of the characters—he's so good at accents—and startling us every time he squeals, "Pieces of eight! Pieces of eight!" Long John Silver is unforgettable, the suspense is unbearable—and by the time the chapter ends, we're way too excited to sleep. We jump up and down on our beds and whack one another with our pillows and shout and yelp and laugh until Desmond interrupts his dinner to read us the riot act.

On weekends, he rents a car and we go for a drive—to the Three Countries' Corner, up the Rhine, into the Schwartzwald, or into France. We've arrived in Colmar, one Sunday, when he pulls over on a city street. It's a summer day, and the car windows are open. I hear another language, which reminds me of the French

Madeleine speaks, but this is more guttural. We pile out of the car, and I discover that Desmond can order a meal in what sounds to me like fluent French.

When I'm home, I'm always with Ian, Brian, and Sheelagh, and it's rare for me to feel special, but that year, on my birthday, Nan and Desmond take me, just me, out to a candlelit restaurant as a treat. Desmond knows someone at the BBC in Basel, and it's about this time that I'm asked to go to a broadcasting studio, where I'm handed a short text to read in English. It's an introduction to a Welsh children's choir singing "O Tannenbaum," which is to broadcast across the UK on December 25 as part of a program about Christmas in different parts of the world.

Granny Jo, hearing the news of my star turn, tunes in on Christmas morning in Belfast, and is disappointed when neither I nor "O Tannenbaum" gets a mention. A year later, my devoted Granny tunes in again, and this time she's thrilled to hear the announcer talk about a little girl who has waited a whole year for this moment— and then to hear my voice all the way from Basel.

Ian and I are packed off to Northern Ireland at the end of the school year. At Heathrow, a British European Airline employee leads us to the gate where we're to board the flight to Belfast. Ian spends the holidays with Daddy's parents, and I stay with Granny Jo and Pappy George, as usual.

I KNOW NOTHING about the work Daddy is doing at Sandoz until one day he brings home a glossy magazine. He is already home when we get in from school, and that never happens. He's impatient for us to gather round, too, and we're curious to see what this is all about.

He opens the magazine on the kitchen table so we can see the photograph splashed across the middle pages. It's an image of a luscious green forest reflected in the still waters of a mountain lake. The sky is blue, the lake is blue, and the reflection of the forest on the mountain is exact, a crisp mirror image. There are two words, only two, at the bottom of the right-hand page: "Mirror calm." Underneath, in the corner, is the Sandoz logo.

That's it.

Desmond is proud. The photograph was taken here in Switzerland, the home of mountains and lakes, stillness and cloudless blue skies. Home of the pharmaceutical industry, too, for Sandoz isn't the only pharmaceutical giant based in Basel; Ciba and Hoffmann-La Roche are here, too. The magazine is for family doctors and psychiatrists, and the photo is an advertisement for the breakthrough drug that Sandoz has developed to allay anxiety.

I study the page, admire the image. It's a photograph, so it must be a real place, but it looks too good to be true. What catches my breath is what I see at the bottom of the page. There's nothing at all about the disorders associated with anxiety, and there is no information on the drug Sandoz is advertising.

Two perfect words. They make me shiver, as though a window is open, letting cool air into the apartment.

This is Daddy's work. As medical director of Sandoz, he's the one responsible for developing and testing the drug, and he's worked with the marketing people on the advertising concept.

"How would anyone know what the drug is called?" I ask.

"There are a few doctors who will want to know that," Desmond acknowledges. "But there's a feature on the drug in this same issue."

"Is there a reason for not mentioning the drug's name?"

"Many people will find that surprising," he says. "And that will pique their interest."

I nod.

"And this drug is so effective," he adds, "that most readers of the magazine already know it and are already prescribing it. So, we don't have to mention it by name. And the image is so much bolder without that."

I can see that. Desmond used to be editor of *Medical World*, after all. He has spent years writing and editing and brainstorming design ideas and illustrations that will attract the attention of doctors. He is the one who knew how effective this ad would be with that photograph. He is the one who knew it would be more effective without the name of the drug. And he is the writer who came up with those two words. My heart is bursting.

HOW DID NAN and Desmond make sense of the way their lives had changed? It was as though they themselves were becalmed—and not because of any mood-altering substance any stronger than whisky. They had cut themselves off even more from their families in Northern Ireland and also, irrevocably, from the communist circles they used to move in. They were entirely out of their element, functioning in a limited way in a foreign country in a language they could neither speak nor understand.

There was much they must have regretted leaving behind. Not the turmoil and the illness, of course not. Not the worry and the rows, not the shock treatment, not the financial hardships, not the rationing, not the smog, and not the delegation of communist women who so memorably paid my mother a visit in Beckenham.

Not even the Communist Party. Desmond must have known that his honesty in talking about the quality of medical care in Romania would mean leaving the party— that was a decision he had made—though he could not have known what all would ensue.

And yet—there had been idealism in those early years, too. They must both have missed that. There had been politics, and they were in the thick of it. There had been comradeship, friendship, love.

Nan had been in love with her communist electrician. What were her regrets?

One thing Desmond surely regretted, when he shut the door on the Communist Party, was leaving *Medical World*.

I had adored his stories about his working life in Bloomsbury, about his meetings with writers and doctors, advertisers and illustrators. About brainstorming sessions, story ideas, cover images. He had kept company with professionals outside the medical world in those days, too—politicians, publishers, other editors, poets, and novelists. He must have loved that.

Of course he loved that. The streets of London had been paved with gold for that young man from Northern Ireland. He made it sound wonderful every time he talked about it.

I HAD THOUGHT it wonderful, too. And now look at that magazine spread. Desmond hadn't left editing behind at all. It had resurfaced in Basel, in full colour, on glossy paper.

This was the life I wanted for myself, when I was a girl—the life of an editor.

It's a life I did eventually make for myself, when I became publisher and editor of a literary magazine thirty years later. Not a *salonnière*; I had never heard the word and had no experience of anything like a literary salon, though that would follow in due course. I was a long way from becoming a writer, too, further still from creating my own publishing house.

All that was in the future. But I did know a little about the life of a magazine editor and the fun to be had in working with others on creating something new. I loved everything I knew about that.

It was a start.

Hampstead

After three years in Basel, we moved back to London, into a garden flat in a large Victorian house in Hampstead. It was the summer of 1959, and I was nine years old.

I had never been in Hampstead before, but it felt familiar enough. The grey skies, the grey stone, the Belisha beacons on Fitzjohn's Avenue, the sliced bread, the tapioca pudding. I don't remember missing Madeleine. I didn't dwell on the past.

I had no further occasion to speak either German or Baslerdütsch; it was as though I had forgotten them altogether.

Which wasn't quite true. I discovered that much later, on a visit to Frankfurt, when German flooded back into my consciousness after a couple of days, and I found myself capable of composing entire paragraphs in a language I had not spoken since childhood.

I WALKED UP Fitzjohn's Avenue and then along Heath Street every morning to Hampstead Parochial School. I was behind in some of the subjects my classmates and I had to prepare for the eleven-plus exam. I didn't feel at home, exactly, but then I hadn't felt at home in Basel, either. I didn't know I would never feel at home again.

My friends were Olivia Sachs, whose family had fled apartheid in Cape Town, and a sweet-faced Dutch girl from Amsterdam named Elsa von Friesen. It felt right that they, too, were from elsewhere, and it felt right that we became inseparable.

I never did get caught up in math, not until we moved to Canada—but I managed well enough in other subjects.

THERE HAD BEEN boys at Sevogel Schule, but boys were in the other half of the school, on the other side of a high brick wall, and had made no impression on me.

I was now at an age to notice and be noticed. This was a mixed blessing, as the boys were friendly and interested, and I had everything to learn.

Jonathan invited me to his birthday, the only girl in a party of six. We played a game in Jonathan's room that resulted in my lying down on the floor in my party dress while the boys inspected me minutely to see if I moved so much as an eyelash. I didn't enjoy that, but it never occurred to me to think there was anything I could do about it.

Mummy, who had given permission for me to go to the party, was shocked to learn I had been the only girl. I thought it better not to mention the game I hadn't liked.

SIMON WAS A good-looking boy with curly brown hair. He liked me, and I liked him, too. We were in the playground after lunch one day when he started punching me on the arm, hard, over and over again. I couldn't get away, as he was holding me against the wall with his other arm.

Nothing like this had ever happened to me, and I didn't know what to say or do. Could I have fought my way out of his grip? Perhaps. I could certainly have yelled out in protest.

I had never learned to fight back. I had never learned to protest; on the contrary, I'd learned it was safer not to let anyone know much at all. I didn't let on when I was sneaky, I didn't let on when I rejoiced, and I especially didn't want anyone, ever, to know when I was hurt.

There was a certain logic to this, in my now eleven-year-old brain. If my foe was hurting me, it was because that's what he wanted to do. It would, therefore, please him to know he had succeeded. Letting on that I was in pain would only encourage him to continue. Much better not to let on.

Simon eventually wore himself out, and I escaped. I said nothing to Mummy when I got home. It didn't seem too important, by that time, and I didn't think she would be interested.

I put on a sleeveless blouse the next morning without noticing that my arm was badly bruised. No one else at home noticed, either, but then Mr. Price saw me in class.

"What happened to you, Linda?" he asked.

I froze. I didn't want to rat on Simon.

It was Vicky Lake who spoke up. "It was Simon who did it," she said. "He punched Linda yesterday in the playground."

Vicky's parents ran the fish-and-chip shop on Hampstead High Street. "Simon fancies Linda," she added.

Mr. Price looked over at Simon, frowning. Then he assigned the class some work to keep us busy.

"Come with me," he said to Simon. "We're going to see the headmaster."

That afternoon, Vicky followed me down the hall, yelling at me because my ponytail was swinging from side to side. I couldn't make sense of any of this, until the day it dawned on me that Vicky fancied Simon.

MR. PRICE WAS tall and incredibly old; he might have been in his late thirties. His jacket was too big for him, and he had a receding chin so that his teeth were seldom visible, which—from what you could see when he opened his mouth to laugh—was just as well. He was bespectacled, with a few long strands of hair combed over his otherwise bald head, and he was the first of my teachers who kept an eye out for me. I noticed that, and I liked it; at home, I was the big, sensible girl who had to keep an eye out for everyone else.

When the time came to write the eleven-plus, Mr. Price walked up and down between the rows of desks. When he came to me, he stopped and read what I had written on the math paper and then, without saying a word, pointed at one line. I looked up at him, then back to the page, where I noticed my mistake and fixed it.

I SELDOM SAW my friends outside school hours. I had been invited to Elsa's flat for tea once, and to Olivia's grandmother's house for Sunday lunch, but as I never invited anyone back—my family hardly ever invited anyone over—that was as far as it went. With charges for every call made, the phone was out of bounds, and I never got used to making calls.

There was no one in all of England who might have visited us, and we saw little of our grandparents, little of my uncle Raymond and his growing family in County Down. Nan was an only child. She and Desmond made no effort to renew old friendships or to make new friends. In part, this was because Nan disliked entertaining, and she loathed the idea of preparing a dinner party.

In the four years we spent in Hampstead, only two people came for dinner, and neither evening went well. Dr. Maurice Pinard had been a colleague of Desmond's in Basel. Over dinner, he expounded on the medicinal powers of garlic, with the result that Nan and Desmond dismissed him as a kook the minute he went on his way. I was helping to serve and clean up, so I heard it all.

The other guest was an old friend named Moira, who was Irish. The wine flowed the evening she came to dinner, but the festivities came to abrupt end after she defended the role played by the Communist Party in the Hungarian Revolution.

She called a few days later to thank Nan for the dinner and invite her to a concert at the Royal Festival Hall. Nan accepted the invitation, but decided in the end not to go, so she sent me instead. I enjoyed the concert, and this was my first visit to the Royal Festival Hall, but Moira was unmarried and childless, with little to say to an eleven-year-old, and I had less to say to her. I was polite, of course, and I thanked her properly when she brought me home, but that was the last any of us ever saw of Moira.

ONCE, WHEN GRANNY Jo was on a visit, she and Nan were out shopping on Hampstead High Street when they happened to meet up with Stanley, the electrician Nan had been in love with years earlier, in another galaxy.

"Stanley went on his way, we only spoke for a few minutes," Nan told me, late in her life, when I visited her in Canterbury.

"So, you introduced Stanley to Granny Jo?" I asked, incredulous,

She said nothing for a bit. "It was upsetting," she said finally.

"Seeing him."

She nodded.

Finally, she said, "Granny Jo had never met him before, of course."

"Of course not."

"But she knew," Mummy added.

"Knew what?"

"She could see I was upset ... she knew there was something about this man that mattered to me."

"She knew he was not any old electrician!"

Mummy almost smiled. "Stanley wasn't any old electrician."

I could hardly contain myself. "So, what happened?"

"We spoke briefly. Then he went on his way."

"Did Granny Jo ask you about him?"

Mummy shook her head.

"Didn't she ask you who he was? What he had meant to you?"

"No. She said nothing. And I said nothing. We finished our shopping and went back to the flat to prepare dinner."

Granny Jo said nothing. Mummy said nothing.

They both felt the powerful emotional bond between Nan and Stanley. They knew it had come to naught. They knew that Nan had not seen Stanley for years, not since long before we moved to Basel. And that they would likely never see each other again.

And neither my mother nor my grandmother said a word.

In the world in which I grew up, this was normal behaviour. And I would have thought this normal, too, once upon a time.

IAN AND I had always been close, without having conversations, exactly, until I became aware that he was developing interests I had never dreamed of. He had been to see one of the Ealing comedies at a cinema near the Belsize Park Tube station, and he had loved it so much that he was dying to tell me. It had never occurred to me to go to a film—that it was possible to decide you wanted to go to the cinema, just like that. What had led him to do such a thing? Did he go alone? I was astonished.

The next time, he took Brian to a film at the Everyman cinema, next door to my school and Brian's. They so enjoyed the film that they stayed on after the screening— and then sat through the whole film a second time. Only then, emerging into the fading light and realizing how late it was, did Ian grab Brian's hand, like Peter Pan, and drag him home for tea.

Ian had become a plane-spotter, too, and I went with him on expeditions to Heathrow, either alone or with Brian. I packed us all a sandwich lunch before we set off, and Ian strapped the binoculars around his neck and tucked a notebook into his pocket. Then we hopped on the Tube for the long ride west and spent the day on the roof of the Queens Building, jotting down the registration numbers and carriers of all the planes we saw.

Ian was at Haverstock Comprehensive School, in Chalk Farm, but Nan and Desmond were unhappy with the school and decided to send him off to Desmond's alma mater, Inst, instead. So, Ian went off to live with Granny Jo and Pappy George.

OUR BOOKSHELVES AT home were lined with Penguins. Orange ones, mostly, as Nan read novels, and green ones, too, as she loved detective fiction; Desmond used to tease her about that. Crime fiction was not quite up to the mark, apparently, and I wondered why that was.

There were Pelican books, too, and blue and purple covers, for Desmond read histories and biographies and essays, which seemed to be more serious than fiction.

Some of the books were recent, for Ian and I were not the only ones who had been short of good reading matter in Basel; Nan and Desmond had reading to catch up on, too. All the Penguin paperbacks used the same colour coding, with a wide band of colour, the book title, and the author's name—George Orwell, Kingsley Amis, Arthur Koestler—on the front cover. On the back was a description of the book and a small, grey-scale photograph of a man—almost always a man—posing stiffly in a suit, a white shirt, and a narrow tie.

I wasn't reading these books, not yet, but I did listen to what Nan and Desmond said about them. I studied the author photos with interest, too. The men looked so ordinary, so dull, and I had expected them to be so magnificent.

Some of the books Nan liked were by women writers. Elizabeth Bowen, Doris Lessing, Muriel Spark, and Iris

Murdoch had their photos on orange Penguins, and Dorothy L. Sayers, Margery Allingham, Agatha Christie, and Ngaio Marsh on green Penguins, clinging by their fingertips to the lower reaches of Mount Olympus. I liked to hear what Mummy said about these books, and I eventually read them all. I studied the photographs of the women, as well. Most of them wore glasses. They all looked old, too, a lot older than Nan, and not half as stylish.

U and Non-U

Basel had been good for me, and London was good, too, though my life in Hampstead was less than mirror calm, mostly because England caused a resurgence of Desmond's complicated feelings about the British class system. That took the form of a wish to pass as an English gentleman. This, on its own, was hardly unusual. As George Bernard Shaw wrote in the preface to *Pygmalion*, there were countless thousands of British men and women who "have sloughed off their native dialects and acquired a new tongue."[3]

Nor is this a historical oddity limited to the postwar years. The writer Zadie Smith, born in 1975, has acknowledged that she herself sloughed off her working-class Willesden accent and replaced it with the posh voice of the Cambridge-educated young woman she became. "I regret it," she writes. "I had hoped to keep both voices alive in my mouth. They were both part of me. But how the culture warns against it!"[4]

My brothers and I were biddable children. If our accents, vocabulary, and manners mattered, it would have been enough merely to let us know what to say and how to behave. Desmond was incapable of doing that. He called us names instead, and he shouted at us when he thought we sounded too Irish and were behaving in ways he found unacceptable.

Desmond's old Bible, back in the day when he was an idealistic young doctor, had been *The Citadel*, a novel by the Scottish doctor A.J. Cronin.[5] Daddy was now a corporate executive, and his new Bible was a blue Penguin entitled *Noblesse Oblige*.[6]

Edited by Nancy Mitford, this slim volume opens with an academic essay on the differences between upper-class—referred to as "U"—and "non-U" English usage. "Today," Birmingham University professor Alan S.C. Ross writes in the opening essay, a member of the upper class is "not necessarily better educated, cleaner, or richer than someone not of this class." It is "solely by its language that the upper class is clearly marked off" from the non-U middle and lower classes.[7]

Ross then explains how upper-class vocabulary and pronunciation identify the speaker as U. "Napkin" is U and "serviette" is non-U. The upper classes say "rich" and the non-U say "wealthy." An upper-class speaker pronounces "girl" to rhyme with "hell."

Noblesse Oblige was fatally interesting to a self-made Irish carpenter's son who was back in London just in time for the book's appearance on the bestseller list. It provided what must have seemed to him like a necessary guide to proper English usage—and to what to avoid if you want to disguise your working-class or regional background. It also poses a crucial question about the possibility of changing one's voice. "Can a non-U speaker become a U-speaker?" Professor Ross asks. The discouraging answer is that "an adult can never attain complete success."

This did not stop Desmond from changing his own voice and Nan's—and all of ours. As he was working during the day, and he and Nan ate dinner alone together, we saw him in the morning, mostly, where he was the autocrat of the breakfast table.

Anything could set him off. A word pronounced in the Northern Irish way, where "garage" sounds like "garridge." Desmond ranted over a mispronunciation of "nuclear" as "nucular," too, and he was outraged if we used a lower-middle-class word like "lounge" instead of "living room."

He had been scrutinizing U table manners, as well, so he didn't limit himself to vocabulary and pronunciation.

We were having boiled eggs one morning when he launched a surprise attack on me. "Not like that!"

I was startled. What did he mean? What had I done wrong? I had cut the top off my egg with my knife, as usual.

Daddy glared at me. He then picked up a teaspoon, and slowly, exaggerating every move, tapped the top of his own egg. We all watched. None of us had ever seen this before.

"You tap it gently," he said. "All around. Like this. And then!"—he slipped the tip of the spoon into the side of the cracked egg, "See! You *scoop* the top off."

Had he been at a breakfast meeting and watched someone do this? Had he read about it?

Desmond scarcely ever used any form of corporal punishment—nothing more than a slipper on the bum—but he used words like darts.

Should I have fought back? How? Is there a universe in which I could have argued this—or any—point with my Napoleonic father?

There is no such universe. That would have been called "answering back." The very idea makes me quake.

I learned my lessons well. And I didn't only learn how to say "gara-a-azhe" in the posh English way. I didn't only learn how to open an egg with a teaspoon. I learned not to fight back, because fighting back made things worse.

ETIQUETTE IS SOMETIMES a trivial subject, and some of the rules of comportment, including the very word "comportment," lend themselves to easy mockery. But etiquette can be admirable.

A 2018 *New Yorker* article on Swiss finishing schools is often condescending towards the young women who trust such schools to teach them how to behave in improbable social situations.[8]

The serious side of etiquette does emerge, though, in what may be an apocryphal story about some guests of Queen Victoria who picked up their finger bowls and drank the contents. The queen's response to this was to drink from her own finger bowl, in order not to embarrass her guests. Whether this story is true or not, it speaks to etiquette as a way of putting other people at ease.

This was not Nancy Mitford's approach. Her contribution to *Noblesse Oblige* disagrees only slightly with Professor Ross's, but she was an aristocrat, unlike him, and hers is the nasal voice of upper-class snobbery. To his analysis, her essay adds a sense of her own superiority that would have further undermined her non-U readers' confidence in the ways they had grown up speaking and acting. And she adds silence to the upper-class arsenal:

> Silence is the only possible U-response to many embarrassing modern situations: the ejaculation of "cheers" before drinking, for example, or "it was so nice seeing you," after saying good-bye. In silence, too, one must endure the use of the Christian name by comparative strangers and surname without any prefix. This unspeakable usage sometimes occurs in letters—Dear xx—which, in silence, are quickly torn up, by me.[9]

I had lots of experience of silence—and good reason to know silence was not limited to the upper crust.

DESMOND WAS CLASS-OBSESSED when he was in class-obsessed England. He had the indignation of a working-class lad from Belfast who'd come up in the world—and the anxiety of a man who was not nearly as confident as he appeared to be.

He and Nan had spent years expunging Irishisms from their own speech. They used to make fun of people in Belfast who talked about a "gateau cake," unaware that "*gâteau*" is simply the French word for cake. They joked about the way Belfast people mispronounced the name Renée as "Reenie." They learned from Mitford to disdain other regional locutions. And of course, they didn't want their children to be sneered at. They wanted us all to move up in the world. So, they meant well. It was for our sakes that they were teaching us what they believed was the right way.

It was for their own sakes, too. Desmond didn't want any of us to betray our Northern Irish background by mucking up the nuances of U-usage. If we were to do that, we might inadvertently betray Nan and Desmond's own non-U background.

What Desmond displayed was anger when he saw me use my knife that morning, but his anger was prompted by anxiety. Just imagine if we were all invited to breakfast by an aristocratic host—Nancy Mitford herself, say. And imagine we were served boiled eggs. And that I betrayed us all by using my knife to slice the top off my egg.

Poor, anxious Daddy. What he needed was someone to calm him down, but no one could do that, not even Nan.

It was not necessary to expunge any hint of our Irishness, and it was not necessary to bully us into behaving in ways Nancy Mitford would have found acceptable. We all became well-spoken and well-behaved, and that would have happened without Desmond's attempts to mold us in Nancy Mitford's image.

Camden School for Girls

It was 1961, I was eleven years old, and I had my first school uniform: a bottle-green tunic, a white blouse, and a blazer with the school crest and the school motto, "Onwards and Upwards," embroidered on the pocket in powder blue thread; for summer, there were green and white gingham dresses. There was a bottle-green Mackintosh with a hood, too, and a bottle-green beret with a cockade in some sturdy synthetic fabric.

Another one of the new girls, Bettina, lived near us in Hampstead, the headmistress told Nan before the start of term. Bettina's mother, who happened to be from Zürich, didn't want Bettina travelling alone on the Tube. Her mother and Nan conferred, with the result that I was invited to tea at their house.

A week or so later, the father, who was the scion of a Scottish earldom, drove Bettina and me to his club for a swim. The very idea of this club was too much for Desmond. When he learned where I was going, his first reaction was to scoff, as he always scoffed at evidence of class privilege. After a few minutes, though, he thought again. "What's the name of this club?" he asked.

"I don't know."

"Do you know where it is?"

"No."

"Let me know," he said. "I might be interested in becoming a member."

THE RESULT OF all this vetting was that Bettina and I met up at the Hampstead Tube station every school-day morning. We never became close friends, but we were the only girls from our school who took the Tube down to Camden Town, where we met up with others before catching the bus to Sandall Road. That's where Bettina and I parted company. Each year was divided into three unimaginatively named classes—1, 1-a, and 1-alpha. I was in 1-a, while Bettina was in 1-alpha, where her close friend was a girl named Gully Wells.

Camden School for Girls was an unusually good school with a clear sense of its mission to educate the daughters of the London intelligentsia and prepare us for university. Bettina was not the only upper-class girl, but most were from middle-class or humble backgrounds; this was a progressive state school with firmly egalitarian intentions.

My class was the one in which the school had grouped all the incoming Jewish girls, which is something the class teacher, two of my classmates, and I discovered when we were the only ones who showed up for class during the Jewish High Holidays.

I lost touch with my classmates when my family moved to Canada in 1963, but I have vivid memories of a few of them. Searching names on the Internet today,

I see that Annabelle Sreberny, a Hungarian girl with an original mind, went on to a distinguished academic career at the School of Oriental and African Studies in London. Another classmate, Nicky Bronowski, was one of four daughters of Jacob Bronowski, a Polish-born mathematician then famous as a television intellectual on *The Brains Trust*. Nicky eventually moved to upstate New York, as I learned when I sat beside her eldest sister, Lisa Jardine—a historian who also became a renowned television intellectual in Britain—when she came to Montreal to accept the inaugural Cundill History Prize at McGill University in 2004.

BETTINA'S GROUP IN 1-alpha was a world apart, both literally and figuratively. Gully, who was the daughter of an American journalist and socialite, went on to Cambridge, where she and Martin Amis dated for a time. She married a television executive, lives in New York, and published a memoir about her childhood, her mother's house in Provence, and their social circle— which included A.J. Ayer, Isaiah Berlin, Iris Murdoch, and Bertrand Russell.[10] The Internet turns up a photo of Bettina in a ball gown taken eight or nine years after I knew her; this accompanies a British newspaper report that she was dating Prince Charles. *Debrett's* notes her marriage to a well-connected Englishman and their current whereabouts.

The plan was for all three classes to move up together until the sixth form. Many went on to university, and several girls—Annabelle and Gully would have been among them—then spent the extra time needed to prepare for admittance to Oxford or Cambridge. I wanted to be one of those girls.

EACH CLASS TOOK turns buying the week's flowers for morning assembly. This was a school tradition that might have been originally inspired by the practical need for someone to go to Covent Garden for the flowers. A well-intentioned headmistress might well have wanted her privileged girls—and we were all privileged girls, regardless of our parents' social standing—to see aspects of daily life in London we might otherwise not see.

My class's turn, that first term, came on a frosty morning in December. I had to get up at dawn, before anyone else was awake, and find my way alone to King's Cross, where I changed to the Piccadilly Line and on to Covent Garden. Bettina and Gully's class had had their turn the previous week; Bettina had not said much about it, but I doubted she had taken the Tube.

I saw no other girls in bottle-green school uniforms on my journey, but I did find my teacher and several classmates at the Covent Garden station, as expected. Others arrived soon enough, up from the Tube or dropped off by a parent. We all then moved into the market, a whole class of pre-teen girls, checking out the flower stands and considering what to buy. The flower sellers were jokey and indulgent with us, though their accents were so thick—some Cockneys, some farm people—that I couldn't follow everything they said.

What had seemed like an odd exercise had turned into an adventure by the time we had chosen our flowers, and we were a proud phalanx of girls bearing flowers aloft as we left Covent Garden. It was still early when we got to school, where our next task was to arrange the flowers in the massive vases on the stage. Whatever the educational value of our expedition, it had been a bonding exercise, which might have been the point. When the bell eventually rang, and we took our seats with the rest of the school, we were convinced the flowers had never looked better.

NAN SPENT A few hours a week working at Pilgrim's Place Antiques on Rosslyn Hill, a short walk from our flat on Prince Arthur Road. She had become a collector and was on her way to becoming a dealer; she wanted to learn the trade and was glad to work in the shop on a volunteer basis. Pietro, the co-owner of the shop, was knowledgeable about English furniture and silver. He later had a position at Christie's, which is where my brother Ian—who works in the photographic archive at English Heritage—ran into him decades later.

I sometimes stopped by Pilgrim's Place after school on the days when Nan was there. It wasn't on the way home, but it wasn't far out of my way, and Pietro was always friendly and chatty.

"I've been telling Nan about the play Donald and I saw last night," he said when I came in one afternoon.

Pietro's partner in the business and in life was Donald West, whom I had seen in the shop from time to time. Older than Pietro, and a taller, rather forbidding man, Dr. West was well-known both as a psychiatrist and as a criminologist. I had heard Nan and Desmond talk about him, as he was the author of *Homosexuality,* a groundbreaking work that argued against the view that gay men could be "cured" or "converted."

"There was a play within the play," Pietro explained. "*Very* interesting."

"Our Shakespeare play this term is *A Midsummer Night's Dream,*" I said. "And I've just come from playing Oberon in a class reading. There's a play within a play there, too."

Nan nodded, but then she had studied the play in school, too. Pietro had grown up in Italy, where class readings of Shakespeare were less common.

"Really!" He was happy to learn this.

"Yes, a play about the love between Pyramus and Thisbe—those are their names. And it's a forbidden love affair. Pyramus and Thisbe live next door to each other and can only communicate through a crack in the wall between them."

"That would be a problem," Pietro said, and we all laughed at that.

It might have been my first literary conversation, outside school.

DR. WEST WASN'T the only writer on the horizon. My parents had stayed in sporadic touch with a few old friends in Northern Ireland—BBC Northern Ireland writer and broadcaster Sam Hanna Bell and the poet W.R. Rodgers along with Alec, the impatient historian on the Antrim coast. I was one of the children, running around outdoors, and I never got to know any writer well until much later on.

There were no classroom visits by authors in those days, and if there were public readings in the public library, or indeed anywhere within reach, I was not aware of them. At home, the radio was on at breakfast time and after school, and Nan used to get the *Daily Express* delivered, though I was indifferent to that.

Desmond picked up a newspaper on his way to work, but which one? The left-wing *Manchester Guardian* would have made sense; permanently estranged though he was from the Communist Party, Desmond was a life-long socialist. He was in disguise in the corporate world, though, so he might have preferred to carry the *Times* around with him.

I had seen celebrity and entertainment magazines in the little shop opposite the Tube station, too, but I had no interest in them, either. I was interested in books.

Dr. Finlay's Casebook

We had always listened to BBC Radio, and the BBC World Service had been our mainstay in Basel, where we had no television, for the good reason that neither Nan nor Desmond would have understood much.

Language was no longer an issue, once we moved to Hampstead, but we still had no television. Did they imagine the quality of programming was poor? Did they have something against television? It was late 1962 when we eventually acquired a set.

I sometimes joined them in front of the television after their dinner, when Brian and Sheelagh were in bed. So, that's how I came to watch the current events show *Panorama*. I saw enough documentaries about the war to provide me with nightmares that have lasted a lifetime. Feature films, occasionally, including at least one horror film that terrified Brian and me late one night when Nan and Desmond had gone out for the evening. And, in 1962 and 1963, the satirical revue *That Was the Week*

That Was, which amused my parents, though I found it incomprehensible.

One program was unlike all the others, though, and that was *Dr. Finlay's Casebook*. I enjoyed this series, and I couldn't help noticing the silence that fell over Nan and Desmond whenever it was on. This was the story of a country doctor in a small Scottish town named Tannoch-brae, where Dr. Finlay's life was similar in many ways to the life that my parents had led early in their marriage.

Nan and Desmond were acutely aware of the similar-ities. In their silence while we watched episodes of the series together, they were thinking of the world they had left behind in Northern Ireland. Ten years had gone by, several of them tumultuous. Nan and Desmond were light years away from the life they had led as newlyweds in Lisburn.

I had no way, in 1962, of knowing the causes of the tumult of the years we spent in Beckenham. If I were only now starting to realize there was a question, I had no way of knowing how long it would take me to find the answer.

Part of the answer would come through books, when I discovered, years later, that the television series was based on a book about the life of a country doctor.

DESMOND HAD LEFT Sandoz and was now working for an American pharmaceutical firm. This didn't last long, for he soon resigned on an issue of medical ethics. This was no doubt an important issue, and Desmond was a doctor of impressive integrity. The lamentable state of medical care in Romania had been important years before, too, important enough to justify the rupture with the Communist Party.

I didn't feel skeptical when I heard Desmond had quit this most recent job in outrage over some ethical lapse; I was too young for skepticism, and I had far too much respect for my father, anyway. I did feel a flicker of unease.

When he was in a good mood, Desmond liked to quote a memorable phrase about "the infinite indignation of the Celt." This may be a phrase written by George Bernard Shaw, an Irishman for whom Desmond had boundless admiration. I suspect he knew the phrase was a good description of some of his own responses.

He and Nan paid a visit to the manager of the Barclay's Bank in Hampstead. We then moved to Devon for several weeks, where Desmond did a locum to bring in some much-needed money. That was the last time he ever practised medicine.

Boobs

I was twelve when I grew boobs. I didn't think of them as boobs at the time. Breasts was the proper name, but that was such an embarrassing word. Boobs were generally embarrassing, no matter what you called them.

We'd all trooped over to Ireland for five weeks in the seaside village of Mullaghmore, County Sligo. Granny Jo and Pappy George came down from Belfast for a visit, as did a medical man who'd been to Queen's with Desmond. Nan wore big shades, splashy sundresses, and strappy sandals. She and Desmond spent most of their time in the lounge bar of Hannan's Hotel, where we were staying.

My memory of the U and non-U battles was still fresh.

"Why is it okay to call this a lounge?" I wanted to know. "Why not a living room?"

One answer was, "Don't be cheeky."

The other was more helpful. "Because this is a hotel."

"Oh?"

"And a lounge is a lounge when it's in a hotel."

THERE WAS A shark in this part of Donegal Bay; I often saw it close to shore. There was a red-faced man, too, known as Barney, who was sometimes referred to, affectionately enough, as the Harbourmaster. My brothers and I spent time near the boats and picked our way towards the lighthouse, scraping limpets off the rocks as we went. We used the limpets as bait for the crabs we caught from the harbour wall and then threw back into the water. On days when we headed in the other direction, towards the beach, we stumbled through reeds and cow pies.

I loved the beach. I'd been swimming for years and was on the swim team at school, though I never came close to winning a race. The beach was sandy and stretched for a mile or more to the Black Rocks. I was often the only one there. Sometimes Sheelagh—not yet six—was with me during the day, and sometimes my brothers. We built sandcastles with wide moats positioned the perfect distance from the water, then waited for the tide to come in.

The moment when the sea rushed into the moat was riveting, as water raced all around the castle and then ebbed. We waited, and it roared back, but there was too much water this time, way too much. The moat was not nearly deep enough to contain it, so of course, it overflowed. The castle collapsed into a lumpy pile of sand, at which point we started all over again, farther up the beach.

Granny Jo and Pappy George came to the beach when they were visiting, but they put towels down on the sand and sunbathed—she in her old-fashioned swimsuit and he in rolled-up trousers and shirtsleeves, with a knotted handkerchief over his bald spot. Everyone paddled in the water to cool off—but I was the one who swam.

"ALWAYS SWIM PARALLEL to the shore," Nan had said. I had almost drowned twice before, the first time out walking in Plymouth Hoe, when I fell into the water unnoticed and was rescued by a man who'd been walking behind us. The second time was in Basel, when I lost my bearings while doing somersaults in the pool, until someone else's daddy set me back on my feet. I didn't know the dangers of a sandy beach.

It was a quiet afternoon, and I was sitting on a towel. Sheelagh was playing in the sand, wearing a cotton sunhat. A honeymooning couple was sunbathing close by, a young soldier and his bride.

I was fascinated by the woman's breast, the one I could see. She was thin, and her swimsuit didn't fit properly. Much of her breast, including her nipple, had slipped out the side. It was almost flat, like a small fried egg, not a bit like my boobs.

I studied this breast, then lay down to see what my own boobs looked like when I was on my back. They did flatten out a bit, but not like a fried egg.

I got to my feet and walked over to the water. I swam parallel to the shore at first, but then, on an impulse, I headed out to sea.

When I stopped swimming and looked back, I was farther from shore than I'd expected. I could see the soldier lying beside his bride; he was on his elbows, watching me. Sheelagh looked small, toiling away with her bucket and spade.

I tried swimming back, then paused to catch my breath. I tried again. I didn't seem to be getting anywhere. I had never heard the word "riptide." I wasn't making any headway, though. That much I did know.

I looked longingly at the shore, tried again to swim back, and still made no progress. Getting alarmed, I waved at the soldier.

He jumped to his feet and ran into the water. It took him less than a minute to reach me, and he pulled me back to safety.

I DIDN'T SAY a word to my parents about this, sure I'd be in trouble if they knew. They had a more pressing matter on their minds, anyway. And there were always things I didn't tell them; I was never sure how they'd react, and I didn't want to anger them. Besides, Desmond, the doctor, made a point of reminding us all that children are very good at surviving; I didn't think he'd be too interested in my escapade.

The honeymooners must not have said anything, either; they, too, were staying at Hannan's Hotel, and we shared the same dining room. There was nowhere else for visitors to stay in Mullaghmore, unless of course you happened to be a guest of Lord Louis Mountbatten, who spent his summers in Classiebawn Castle, at the top of the escarpment. We saw him once, pushing off from the harbour in a boat filled with young relatives.

"Fenders in, boys!" he ordered, in the plummiest voice I have ever heard.

It was in Mullaghmore harbour, almost twenty years later, that his boat was blown up by the Provisional IRA, killing him and several members of his family.

THE PRESSING MATTER that was preoccupying Nan and Desmond was that Marilyn Monroe had died. She had taken an overdose of barbiturates and had been found dead in her bed.

"Suicide" was a new word to me, and I could see that my parents were in a state of shock, more upset than I had seen them in years. I hadn't realized they cared that much about Marilyn Monroe, though I did know who Marilyn Monroe was.

I also knew that Desmond thought Marilyn Monroe was sexy. Nan must have thought so, too. She would not have dreamed of dying her auburn hair blonde, but she had taken to wearing her hair in a similarly soft, wavy style. My mother was lovelier than ever, that summer. Her body had always been both trim and curvaceous, and she was flaunting it more than usual. Her sundresses had plunging necklines that showed off her breasts, and her high-heeled sandals drew attention to her legs.

Sexy. Nan looked sexy.

"Sexy" wasn't an entirely new word to me, but it was a word that had only now acquired meaning. I studied the photographs of Marilyn Monroe in the *Irish Times* and listened in on my parents' conversations in the lounge bar with more than my usual concentration.

IT'S LIGHT UNTIL late, in summer in Ireland, and Hannan's Hotel served the evening meal early. I headed back to the beach on my own after dinner. Not to swim, for it was cooler now, and I'd done all the swimming I was going to do; I adored the long walk out towards the Black Rocks at the far end of the beach. Granny Jo came with me while she was visiting. This was a coast she remembered from her own childhood, when her grandfather had been the Mullaghmore coast guard. She was not happy with my solitary walks, though. "You shouldn't come out here on your own," she told me.

"There's no danger," I said. "There's no one here, ever."

"You can't be sure of that."

"I like being on my own," I added.

It was the solitary nature of these walks that appealed to me most of all. That and the softening light. And there was no one I particularly wanted to accompany me, except Granny Jo.

SHE WAS RIGHT, though. It was after Granny Jo and Pappy George had headed back to Belfast that I became aware that red-faced Barney, the so-called Harbourmaster, had started following me. He stayed hidden, so I didn't know at first that he was creeping around in the rushes, and I paid him no attention when I did notice him. I had no reason to think he posed any kind of threat.

And then, one night, he approached me, lurching and groping. I was young and fit, and he was an old drunk. I got away easily, unscathed.

He did have an effect, though. He spoiled those long walks for me. I never went to the beach alone after dinner again.

Latin Lessons

Nan was always able to help me when I had difficulty at school. I had managed well enough in French, in my first year at Camden School for Girls, but not nearly as well as classmates who spoke the language fluently. Gully might have been the only one whose family owned a house in France, but she was not the only one who spent time there.

Latin became my favourite subject, and here the playing field was even, for none of us had learned Latin before. I loved learning how the language worked, its structure, its syntax, its declensions, its conjugations, and especially its vocabulary. I even loved the exceptions to all the rules, which added to the challenge. I was thrilled to learn the origins of so many English words and delighted by the way that differences between English and Latin illuminated English for me. What I loved most was translating short passages from Latin to English. That meant taking Latin texts I had understood little, if at all, when I first read them, and making sense of them.

What a pleasure! I had never had such fun, not in school, not anywhere. Translation gave me a power I had not known I was capable of. I was good at translating Caesar, who was easy, if shocking, with his accounts of hostage-taking, torture, beheadings, and other cruelties—all of which seemed so remote and alien that I was certain they could have no bearing on the modern world into which I was growing up.

The Latin teacher, Miss Bew, enjoyed this part of her job, too, I could see that, and she passed her love of the language and of translation on to me. Miss Bew was like a character from a Barbara Pym novel—wiry, stern, idiosyncratic, admirable. I admired her authority, her knowledge of ancient Rome and Roman life, and her sureness about the meaning of Latin words. There was something so clean and pure about Latin.

I enjoyed Catullus, especially, and Martial's epigrams. It was play, trying to find the right words, the right combination of words, struggling to make my translation as concise and exhilarating as the original. Getting inside the text created an intimate connection between me and the writer. It felt like the most intimate connection possible.

I had never minded homework, but I had never before known the joy I felt when our homework was to translate a poem. I worked on my translation for hours, scrapping early versions, starting over, tweaking it again and again.

I was delighted, too, by the snippets of biographical information Miss Bew passed on to the class when she was introducing a writer. I loved hearing about the writers' lives, which were a revelation. I had never known a writer well enough to consider that they might have experienced jealousies and sorrows. The very idea of their having lives fascinated me, and it didn't occur to me to think about how long these Latin authors had been dead.

Latin was the language of ancient Rome and much of its empire, and there were no ancient Romans around anymore. They were all dead, and their language had been Latin, *ergo* their language was dead. But dead was a word that didn't seem right. The writers and their language felt alive to me.

We didn't speak Latin in class, not in order to converse, and Miss Pym never used Latin in her teaching, except when quoting from a text. We certainly never wrote in Latin. Latin was a language we worked with, doing exercises, learning vocabulary, reading, and translating. Whenever Miss Bew and the class talked about authors or their work, we spoke in English. Latin was not a language we ever used as language is normally used, to communicate with others and express ourselves.

There was just one exception.

I WAS FEELING proficient, in my second year of Latin. Finishing a test early one day, and feeling cheeky, I wrote, "*O me miseram!*" at the bottom of the page. Oh, wretched me!

Why did I do this? I knew I had aced the test, so I wasn't complaining. Far from. I was strutting, proud to show Miss Bew that I wasn't limited to grammar and vocabulary and translation. I was using Latin to express myself.

Without being conscious of this, I was also proving that Latin wasn't dead, after all, at least not to me. I was using Latin as a writer uses a living language. I was nearly thirteen, with the unbounded intellectual confidence of a clever adolescent girl, and I thought my ironic little note would amuse Miss Bew.

O me miserum is the masculine, and those are the original words written by Cicero, one of the authors we had been reading. I knew I had to use the feminine ending—*miseram*—when speaking for myself. I was pleased with myself for the allusion to Cicero, and I was sure Miss Bew would be pleased with me, too.

SHE STORMED INTO class next day, her face flushed and mottled.

"There is a girl in this class," she announced, "who has had the temerity to turn yesterday's test into a laughing stock."

My classmates and I exchanged mystified glances.

"When there is a test," Miss Bew went on, her voice as crisp as burnt toast, "I expect my girls to take it seriously."

I tensed up, reminded of my little in-joke, but Miss Bew wasn't looking at me; she was looking at everyone other than me.

"Education is a privilege," Miss Bew continued. "It is not to be taken lightly. You are old enough to be aware of that. I design a test to make sure you are learning what you need to learn in order to continue your studies. I do not expect you to add a joke at the end of the test paper."

She paused, looked from girl to girl, at every girl but me. Then she whirled to face me. "Why did you do it, Linda?"

I had shrunk into my hard wooden chair, speechless. "I expect better of you, Linda."

IT WAS SUCH a small transgression, if it was a transgression at all. She gave me a zero on the test, to teach me.

And what did that teach me?

It taught me to shut up, mostly, which was something I didn't need to learn. I had spent most of my life keeping quiet.

It taught me to beware of someone in a position of power, too. Another lesson I didn't need.

And it taught me something else. I had had great faith in Miss Bew, and I couldn't understand why she had reacted with such anger. I had disappointed her—yes, I understood that, sort of. I had enraged her. I certainly hadn't intended to do that. I hadn't known I could do that. I thought I had done something special.

Miss Bew had overreacted; I knew that. And Miss Bew was the one with the power to humiliate and punish. But why did she want to do that? She had never been a teacher who kept an eye out for me, as Mr. Price had done, but I loved Latin, and Miss Bew had certainly noticed how much attention I lavished on my translations.

There was something behind the disappointment and the rage, and I had no way of knowing what that was. It was a lesson in the mysteries of human behaviour.

IT WASN'T MUCH of a start at writing, just three allusive words in Latin with a change of gender and a whiff of irony. I didn't think of it as writing at the time, and it's a stretch to call it that now. But it was a step towards communicating in my own voice, in speaking for myself, even if it was in a language that was not my own. Perhaps because it was in a language that was not my own.

If writing can get you into trouble, as those three words in Latin got me into trouble with Miss Bew, this little episode was a first lesson in the dangers of writing.

3.
The Napoleonic Wars

Children begin by loving their parents; as they grow older they judge them; sometimes they forgive them. —OSCAR WILDE, *The Picture of Dorian Gray*

Montreal

We were travelling first class, courtesy of Pfizer Canada, which had hired Daddy as medical director. On our first night out, we sat down to dinner in the vast dining room, where the staff heavily outnumbered the few guests. I seldom wore dresses, but Nan had bought me a flouncy powder-blue number to wear for such occasions. My boobs were growing so fast, though, that I was already bursting out of this dress and attracting unwanted attention.

So, I wasn't unhappy to flee back to the stateroom when I felt seasick. By the next day, the *Carinthia* was caught in the aftermath of a North Atlantic storm, and I spent the rest of the ocean voyage in bed, returning to the dining room only when we reached the Gulf of Saint Lawrence. I never wore that dress again.

THE HOLIDAY INN on chemin de la Côte-de-Liesse was our home until the furniture arrived. The Pfizer office was nearby, so Daddy went off to work while the rest of us spent hot summer days outdoors by the pool. It was a scorching July morning when we moved out of the Holiday Inn and piled into our lumbering Pontiac Parisienne. We headed south and west of Montreal to Pointe-Claire village, where we saw nuns on the Lakeshore Road and two girls about my age. With my eye out for new friends, I checked out their shiny hair, their pale summer shorts and T-shirts, their sandals, their bare arms and legs. I had not been slow, in the past, to make friends after a move, but I never did see those sandalled girls again.

Golf Avenue, west of the village of Pointe-Claire, runs between Beaconsfield Golf Club and the graceful wooden houses built about 1910 on the solid rock of the Canadian Shield. The one Desmond had rented for us was white with green trim, with a vast veranda overlooking the pond on the 18th fairway.

THE MORE I settled into my Canadian life, the more I was at sea. The adolescent lurch towards adulthood was part of this, as were battles with my father. The dearth of public transport on the Lakeshore meant I spent more time at home than ever before, and there were distances I never learned to cross.

Though I knew most of the words spoken in Canadian English, there were times I had difficulty understanding their meaning. Where I said nappies, Canadians said diapers; where I talked about the lavatory, the lav, or the loo, they talked about the washroom. Some of the expressions I used—laying the table, knocking her up—caused me embarrassment, and some words were pronounced or spelled in ways that were unfamiliar.

Canadian English was far from a new language, but I did find myself stumbling over Canadian expressions and pronunciation. Though hardly a big issue, this served as a reminder that I was from somewhere else. My sons love to tease me to this day about the way I pronounce words like "mall" and "palm."

The international French I learned at Beaconsfield High School was in some ways more familiar, but one odd legacy of the German I had learned in Basel was that I spoke French with a German inflection, so I sounded foreign in French, too. I sound like a native speaker of German, when I can muster a few words in that language, but those few words are all I have.

Mavis Gallant has said that her history of displacement after her father's death meant that there was no context that she didn't understand immediately. I had difficulty believing this, for my own experience was so different. I understood very little, even when I knew the language, whatever language it was.

BEACONSFIELD HIGH SCHOOL was disciplinarian, in 1963, and dull. I was behind my classmates in Latin and in French, and ahead in mathematics, all of which puzzled me, for different reasons.

My new classmates had not studied Latin for any longer than I had—the same two years—so how could they know more than I did? As I soon learned, though, we never read Latin texts in class at BHS, and we never spent time on translation. Perhaps the time my new classmates had not spent on Catullus and Cicero had been time spent on grammar. In any event, I caught up soon enough.

I was doing crazily well in mathematical subjects, to my great surprise, routinely getting grades of 100 percent in algebra and geometry—and not only in Grade 9 but up to and including the final exams at the end of Grade 11. This was not thanks to any new aptitude of mine; I just happened to have covered the very same material in London years before.

FRENCH WAS THE real mystery.

I had studied French for two years in London, whereas French had been a compulsory subject for my new BHS classmates for five years, since Grade 4, and there wasn't one of them who could frame a sentence of more than four words. What had they been doing all this time? Why did they know no more French than I did?

This ineptitude was part of a far bigger mystery. There was a whole French-speaking world here in Quebec, yet we heard not a word of Quebec French at Beaconsfield High School. The vast majority of Quebec francophones were Roman Catholic, and Catholic teachers were permitted to teach in Catholic schools, but not in Protestant schools like BHS. A few of our French teachers were Protestant immigrants from France, and others were Jewish or Muslim immigrants from French-speaking parts of the Middle East and North Africa.

Most of us didn't learn Quebec French on the street, either. Our own neighbours on Golf Avenue were English-speaking, as were most of my classmates' neighbours in Beaconsfield, Beacon Hill, and Beaurepaire. Most of the families in Pointe-Claire village itself were francophones, though, as were those in other long-established communities along the Lakeshore, and there was little mingling between what really were worlds apart. When the two did meet—in the IGA grocery store in the village, say, or in the post office—francophones customarily spoke English to their anglophone customers.

OUR FRENCH TEACHERS were limited to *explications de texte*, exercises, and occasional writing assignments. No mention was made of what was happening in Quebec—and this at the height of the Quiet Revolution, when the province was in ferment. The textbook that provided our only reading included neither fiction nor poetry, and such conversation as there was in class was desultory and awkward.

There can have been few more discouraging jobs than teaching French to English-speaking West Island kids in those years. As I eventually realized, the main reason my classmates knew no more French than I did was that they had no interest in speaking French and could see no reason to bother. That wouldn't begin to change until after the Parti Québécois was elected in 1976, and the passage, the following year, of what Anglos still call Bill 101, the law that regulates the use of English in the province.

SO, I WAS an oddity, with my reserve, my English accent, and my odd expressions. I didn't look like the other girls, either. Lots of them had long hair, but few wore it in a ponytail, and those who did softened the effect with what I was learning to call "bangs." None wore their hair pulled back straight off their faces, as I did, until I bowed to local fashion and had a haircut, which, I quickly discovered, required me to spend time fixing my hair every morning.

My body was still changing, too, and I was physically self-conscious. I used to watch the cheerleaders practise their routine in the school lobby, chanting and twirling and leaping into the air. These were the popular girls who had boyfriends on the football team. I wished and *wished* I were one of the cheerleaders. I envied them their grace, their neat little figures, their easy camaraderie, and their boyfriends.

In years of awkwardness, the most awkward moment of all, both for Mummy and for me, was the little talk we had when I started menstruating. She was matter-of-fact about the man putting his penis into the vagina. This was news to me, and these were words I'd never heard. My face must have registered my disbelief.

She looked at me, and to her everlasting credit, she added, "It's fun."

OUR FRENCH TEACHER assigned homework requiring us to write about our weekend. I had spent that weekend, like every other weekend, babysitting, peeling vegetables, washing dishes, and watching whatever Desmond wanted to watch on TV. I read, too, when I could get away with that, out of sight.

I was far from being able to say anything true about myself or my life, so I knew I had to make something up. But what? I cast about and finally decided I'd write about curling.

I had never been curling, I hardly knew what curling was, but I'd seen it on television from time to time and figured this was what Canadians must do. Curling would surely make for a plausible story.

When he returned the assignments in class, the French teacher was laughing. Laughing at me. He knew I'd made it all up.

If I wanted to keep myself to myself, I realized, I'd have to do a better job of storytelling.

THE SCHOOL BUS did not come up Golf Avenue, so Ian and I cut through our back yard to the bus stop on the next street, de Breslay Avenue. He and I sat together every morning and every afternoon, saying little to the other students and less to each other. We were both introverted and I, for one, was unhappy.

There was a public marker of our difference, too, for our house was unlike any other in Pointe-Claire—unlike any other house anywhere in Canada, no doubt—for it had two life-sized marble busts outside the front door. These were of eighteenth-century British statesmen Sir William Pitt the Younger and Sir Percival Spencer, who surveyed the golf course imperiously from the top of our front steps. Among the antiques Nan had acquired in London, these stony Englishmen had found a new perch here on Golf Avenue. In winter, their heads and shoulders were draped in snow.

I started writing poetry.

MUCH HAD CHANGED in the months since we crossed the Atlantic. Granny Jo had flown over to live with us after she had settled her affairs in Belfast. We were now a household of eight people, ranging in age from Granny Jo, now in her sixties; Nan and Desmond, forty-one and forty-two; Ian and I, fifteen and thirteen; as well as

Brian, eleven; Sheelagh, seven; and almost one-year-old Mandy. In our last years in London, when Ian had been at school in Belfast, and before Mandy was born, there had been only five of us living in our snug apartment in Hampstead.

A household of eight requires a lot of shopping, a lot of cooking, a lot of cleaning, and a lot of managing. Desmond didn't want Nan to be burdened with domestic duties. He had come a certain distance in life by this time. Having made good after the roller coaster of the early 1950s, he enjoyed being the lord of the manor. That meant that his lady should lead a life of leisure. Which was all very well, except that a life of leisure was realistic only if there were servants doing the work.

Wil, our chatty Dutch cleaning woman, came in to scrub upstairs and down, but there was far more to do than she could accomplish in two days a week. That's where the rest of us came in.

Granny kept busy with knitting, mending, babysitting, and sundry kitchen duties. Ian and Brian got to help outside in the garden, which was enormous, with an expanse of grass to cut in summer, piles of maple leaves in autumn, and sensational snowdrifts in winter. Desmond bought himself a second-hand Jaguar that required endless attention, some of which Ian learned to provide.

I WAS AS willing a helper as ever, but there was no end to what needed doing. I got that Nan and Desmond depended on me to keep some of the wheels of the household turning; that had not changed. My father was increasingly volatile, however, and the history of his mental illness would have been very useful information for me to have. An awareness that families could be dysfunctional would have helped, too.

There was no one I could turn to. Not Ian, and not Granny Jo, the other targets of Desmond's wrath. Dependent as Granny Jo now was on his largesse, she didn't dare speak up.

And especially not Nan. When I confided my unhappiness to her, she told Desmond I had complained, which was the start of another row. I felt powerless, and the story of Cinderella looked like realism to me.

MY DUTIES WERE both varied and unending, for the list of tasks I was responsible for consisted of everything that needed to be done. Nothing was ever defined, and nothing was ever enough.

A servant requires her employer, a housekeeper, or a butler—someone in charge—to tell her what to do. Desmond was at work five long days a week and didn't necessarily know what needed doing. He didn't want Nan to have to tell me, either; he didn't want her to have to give it any thought at all. I was expected to figure it out for myself. He would have been delighted if Granny Jo had taken on the managerial role, but that was not a role she was suited for.

Unlike Nan, Desmond had never trained as a teacher. His approach to educating us was his Sunday sermon, when he was in a good mood; at other times, he shouted and inflicted pain—hectoring and mocking us, insulting us and calling us names. Some of the names he called me were vile, most of them were humiliating, and a few of them, now that I think of it, were not bad, barbed though they always were—as when he called me "the Duchess" and Granny Jo "the Dowager Duchess."

Being the eldest girl in such a big family was the worst position to be in. It was never going to be enough that I just prepare the bloody carrots. What was required was *anticipatory* helpfulness. I was expected to know that we'd be having carrots with our dinner, peel them, put them on to boil at the right moment, keep an eye on them, drain them, clear the kitchen counter, set the table—and then imagine what else could possibly be needed before we could all sit down. And do that, too.

Desmond was convinced I was slacking off, so I did everything I could think of doing. It was impossible to predict what might anger him, though, and impossible to know when enough was enough. It was impossible not to be anxious.

So, I did what needed to be done, and then I did more, so that there was no domestic chore Nan would have to concern herself with. And I took great care to do it all cheerfully. If I looked the least bit unhappy, Desmond told me I had the face of a "sick spaniel." Not the most terrible thing—he'd called me nastier names, like "slut" and "slattern"—but it was enough to teach me to become practised at disguising everything I thought and felt.

I had no good strategy. One day, I would escape.

MY ROOM WAS a mess, admittedly, and I had managed to resist repeated appeals to tidy it up. Given how much else I did, this didn't seem to me a terrible sin. Not enough to justify Desmond's rage, surely.

Not *that* much rage.

I was out on a date one night—one of exactly two dates I had in my three years at Beaconsfield High School—when Desmond stormed into my room and pulled out every single drawer, emptied every cupboard, tore posters off the wall, stripped the bed, and flung all my belongings around the room.

When I got home, I crept upstairs, hoping not to waken anyone.

Were they really all asleep? The house was dark and ominously quiet. I was late, but not *that* late, I told myself.

My room looked as though a bomb had gone off in it.

The rage that prompted such violence terrified me. And why was everyone so silent now? No one could have slept through the tornado that had wrecked my room.

I cleared enough space to get to the bed, found my pillow and the blanket under piles of clothing and shoes and books, and climbed into bed, shaking.

The silence the next morning was worse. No one seemed to know anything about what had happened. Desmond had nothing to say to me then, or for days to come. I did my best to stay out of his way.

The tension mounted. Something else was going to happen, but I couldn't tell when—or what. All I knew was that I had no way of preventing it. I retreated into a sullen silence of my own, which further infuriated Desmond—and led to the next storm.

I started pulling out my eyebrows.

I HAD NO right to complain. No rights of any kind, in fact, not when Desmond demeaned me, not even when he destroyed the application I had prepared for an Avon scholarship. This was the generous scholarship offered to a top graduating student on the West Island, where Avon Canada was based. Knowing I stood a good chance of getting the scholarship, I spent a lot of time on my application.

Sometime after I'd given Daddy the envelope to mail—he mailed all our letters from the office—I mentioned at breakfast that I'd received no acknowledgement from Avon.

He flicked a glance in my direction. "I tore the application up," he said.

"What?" I could hardly believe my ears. That scholarship had been my ticket to freedom!

He knew that. That was the reason he'd trashed it.

We were in the kitchen, and he had a glass in his hand. He took a sip, eyeing me like a grizzly bear.

I was shaking. The air seemed made of rotten eggs.

Emboldened by astonishment and fury, I asked, "Why did you do that?"

This was answering back, a cardinal sin.

He flung the contents of his glass in my face. The liquid was ice cold, and it tasted odd, like licorice. I saw the bottle sitting on the kitchen counter. It was Pernod.

I wiped my face on my sleeve and fled.

SILENCE HAD ITS own perils, for silence meant I was sulking, and sulking was forbidden. Feeling sorry for myself was forbidden. Speaking out, complaining, protesting, remonstrating, answering back, having the face of a sick spaniel—all forbidden. The punishment for any infringement was swift. Flinging Pernod in my face is a questionable educational practice, but shockingly effective. And it had to be Pernod; there may be no drink harder to forget.

Was this a reign of terror?

No. It was no such thing. This was one big, happy family—and don't you forget it. Nan was supposed to be a lady of leisure, and the rest of us were supposed to feel blessed by the wonderful life Desmond had provided us with.

HE HAD SHOUTED in London, too. What was new was not his anger; it was the increasing frequency, ferocity, and unpredictability of his anger.

He fought me tooth and nail when I was fourteen and fifteen, and he became desperate to keep me at home when it became increasingly clear that I longed to get out. Though my contribution to household tasks was one reason he wanted to keep me around, there was another, deeper reason.

The family, the house we lived in—that mad outpost of empire on Golf Avenue—was his world. This was the world he and Nan had created, the hub of their universe. He and Nan had a few acquaintances—one or two people he worked with, antique dealers Nan was getting to know—but no real friends. No one knew my parents' story, and that was the way they wanted it. They had each other, they had us, they had a couple of fancy cars, and they had a house full of antiques, with Pitt and Percy on sentry duty at the front door.

The family was important to me, too, all too important. I had made friends at school, but they lived miles away, the only local bus was the school bus, and I had never gotten used to the telephone, so we had no contact outside of school.

In tearing up the Avon scholarship application, Desmond had torn up my best hope of escape.

I did know I'd eventually break out of jail, but how?

TO COMPLICATE MATTERS further, Desmond was as charming as he had always been, and every bit as charismatic.

Sunday dinners were the best and the worst of times. We set the big Hepplewhite dining table with the silver and the good china, lit candles in the candelabra, and set out the pressed glass goblets.

Nan came downstairs in green satin hot pants with white go-go boots. Full makeup, hoop earrings, and long, polished nails. Desmond took charge of the roast in the oven while Nan sipped her gin and tonic.

I was head server, when it was time to sit down. Desmond declared himself satisfied with his expertise in the kitchen and exclaimed that the beef—or lamb, or pork, or fowl—was the best ever. He then moved into lecture mode, recounting stories about man's injustice to man—distant wars, Russian serfs, coal miners in Welsh villages, and the Irish famine. The fact that more people died of disease in wartime than were ever killed by enemy fire. George Bernard Shaw and Winston Churchill and Rommel the Desert Fox. He was holding forth, yes, but he was also doing his best to teach us what he knew and what he'd learned from his reading.

Many of the stories were spine-chilling, and Desmond told them well. I, for one, accepted his word as the whole truth and nothing but the truth, and it was years before I discovered he was wrong about some of the details. About the big picture—the cruelty of those in control, the courage of those fighting for change, man's inhumanity to man—he was never wrong.

Lord Acton was one of the great men he loved to quote. "Power tends to corrupt," he said, "and absolute power corrupts absolutely." Did he not see himself in this? Was he not aware that he wielded absolute power over all of us? From where I sat, Desmond looked like the king of the castle.

Sometimes, he was entertaining. When the dinner had been fine, and he was unusually expansive, he told a joke or two, which he did brilliantly, with his unerring sense of timing and a talent for putting on his characters' accents and voices.

In his youth, he had played Rosencrantz in a school production of *Hamlet*, wearing—we'd all seen the cast photos—a velvet suit, shoes with silvery buckles, and a wide-brimmed hat trimmed with white ostrich feathers. It was a rare Sunday night when he started mimicking his younger self, pushing his chair back from the table and getting to his feet to show us the exaggerated bow he had perfected for the part.

Whatever the tale, whatever the mood, it was our job to listen and appreciate—and laugh when it was time to laugh. Never to argue. Never to say a word, in fact. These were sermons and performances, not seminars. There were no questions and no conversations.

The Victorian dictum that children should be seen and not heard applied not only to the five of us—and to Granny Jo, in the years she spent with us; it applied to Nan, too. She listened, nodded, and occasionally smiled, but she had no more to say than the rest of us.

Should any hint of dissension interrupt Desmond's delight in the occasion—if one of us didn't like the bloody slice of lamb, say, or the beef tongue that was the evening's pièce de résistance—his mood darkened, and the shouting began. It was always a relief when the meal came to an end without incident.

Except, except—sometimes, he would start singing sentimental Irish songs. The one he loved best had lyrics by the poet Thomas Moore:

> Believe me if all those endearing young charms
> Which I gaze on so fondly today
> Were to change by tomorrow and fleet in my arms
> Like fairy gifts fading away
> Thou wouldst still be adored
> As this moment thou art
> Let thy loveliness fade as it will
> And around the dear ruin each wish of my heart
> Would entwine itself verdantly still.[11]

Nan smiled at him, smiled at us all, and opened her arms graciously to accept the compliment. We smiled, too. For all the ups and downs of his days, of Desmond's life, Nan was always adored. That was the real rock on which his castle was built.

THERE WERE PRESSURES on the corporate ladder—Desmond was promoted to vice-president of Pfizer in 1964—and we were his refuge from those pressures. We were all adored, collectively, as a family—and we knew that, even though I, for one, didn't feel adored.

In his forties, well established in his corporate career, Daddy had put on a few pounds, which accentuated his resemblance to Napoleon, of whom a dark, sombre portrait hung on the living room wall. Daddy had bought a dental prosthesis, too, to replace the front tooth he'd lost to a cricket ball in his youth, so he looked less dangerous than he really was.

Less dangerous, but no less eccentric. The whole time we lived in Canada, he continued to wear the stiff white paper collars he ordered in bulk from Austin Reed of Regent Street. Every weekday morning, he would take one out of the box it had arrived in and button it to the top of his collarless shirt. Crisp as it was when he put it on, the paper had softened by the time he got home, especially in the wilting heat and humidity of the Montreal summer.

Popular in the Victorian and Edwardian eras, these collars had been anachronistic long before the 1960s. They are available today on eBay, which describes them as "vintage." The sartorial equivalent of the marble busts at our front steps, Desmond's collar was a daily declaration to Canadians that he was proud to be British—and proud to stand out from the crowd.

HIS PSYCHIATRIC HISTORY and his past membership in the Communist Party lurked in the background, never mentioned. Exposure of either one might well have scuppered his career and all our lives.

I was fourteen, and Ian was fifteen, when Desmond announced he was driving down to New York and wanted us to go with him, which meant taking us out of school for several days. He offered no explanation, and we knew better than to ask questions.

When we were getting close to the border, Desmond told us we should be sure not to mention his affiliation with the Communist Party. That was an unnecessary warning, for we had been told next to nothing and were, in any event, well schooled in saying nothing. As he had always avoided all mention of his communist past, the surprise was that he had now raised the subject.

I didn't know then that anyone who had been a communist was denied entry to the United States. Airports were the worst—especially international airports, which had voluminous documentation at hand—and trains and buses could be risky. The safest way was to drive and take a quiet crossing from rural Quebec into upstate New York. Especially if you were a white suburban dad travelling with his teenage kids.

Desmond would have done anything not to cross the border at all, but he had not been able to get out of the big Pfizer meeting that was coming up. Ian and I were with our subversive father in order to make him look innocent.

It worked. We crossed into upstate New York without difficulty and checked into a hotel in Midtown Manhattan at the end of the day. Desmond had a Pfizer reception and a dinner to attend that evening, then meetings over the next couple of days. He handed Ian some U.S. dollars and left us to our own devices.

Ian was in charge, as he always was when he and I travelled together. He's the one who negotiated the subway, he's the one who led us to the top of the Empire State Building, and he's the one who found us a diner and then, for our lunch the next day—he did not lack for daring—a Japanese restaurant full of serious gentlemen in business suits. There we removed our shoes, as instructed, and, with little experience of international cuisine—we'd never so much as tasted pizza, let alone Asian dishes—we sat across from each other at a low table, picked up the chopsticks provided, and ate food we didn't recognize as food.

SO, IAN AND I knew a little of the political history, but the diagnosis of manic depression had been so closely guarded a secret that Nan was the only one who knew about it, and she kept the story to herself for years after Desmond died.

Would it have done me any good to know?

Knowing about his diagnosis might have troubled me. Desmond could be frightening, and it's possible that knowing about his history of mental illness might have been more frightening.

But his behaviour with me was already disturbing. I just couldn't identify what I'd done to deserve it.

I wish I had known the truth. It might have allowed me to understand what was bewildering, and it would certainly have provided me with some of the words I lacked.

Knowing the truth would also have allowed me to feel some sympathy for Daddy at a time when I felt so unfairly targeted. And for Mummy, too, who must have recognized some of his symptoms and been alarmed. Acknowledging what was happening would have made it possible for us to talk about it, too.

Who am I kidding? Knowing the truth would have meant having an entirely different family.

For this was my family, for good and ill. There was so much that was good, even marvellous, so much that was not good at all. These were the only parents I had, the only ones I would ever have, and—isolated as we always were from other families—the only ones I had ever known.

To the extent that I knew them.

AND IF I had had the words I needed? Who would I have spoken to? Nan had planted her flag beside Desmond's. Talking with Desmond himself was inconceivable. There was some powerful charge surging through him, and I got electrocuted every time I went close.

Granny Jo was uneasy. I was anxious. My brothers and sisters each have their memories, their own stories.

As Desmond aged and became less bombastic, more depressed, we each had a different father.

Ian and I were the eldest and the closest in age, so we had shared more of Daddy's heyday than the others, over a longer time, but even our experiences differed. All five of us lived through the tensions, the lectures, and the hilarity of life on Golf Avenue, though it was impossible to make sense of what we knew.

One of my most vivid memories of that time is of silence, and this was a silence I found oppressive. I often felt alone in that crowded house with my parents, my siblings, and poor Granny Jo. She had only a widow's mite, but she did have the advantage of being an adult, which looked like an enormous advantage to me. Eventually she decided she'd rather be back in Northern Ireland.

Mr. Baker

What I needed was a refuge. Though Beaconsfield High School wasn't a patch on Camden School for Girls, it was my lifeline, and it improved immeasurably when a new teacher, Patrick Baker, arrived to teach history and English when I was starting Grade 10.

Mr. Baker was the best teacher I ever had, in any subject, and the tallest, thinnest man I ever met. I had befriended a couple of other girls who were writing, and Mr. Baker, who was their English teacher but not mine (he taught me history), arranged for an empty classroom where my friends and I could meet after school.

I had started writing stories and short essays as well as poems, in English and sometimes in French. I was writing not in order to mislead, as I had tried so foolishly to mislead my French teacher in Grade 9. I had begun to experiment with ways of saying something true. I had no great preference for this style over that, and not much idea of what style was. Some of what I wrote was long and wordy, but then I started writing epigrams, which I worked hard on, and which appeared in school publications. They strike me now as both serious and naively old-fashioned. Here is one:

> The purpose of life is to find
> The purpose of life.

I must have thought I could solve the riddle of the universe if only I could put the right words in the right order. Here is another:

> If man could see that those who died on the
> battlefield died in vain,
> They did not die in vain.

It's hard to imagine any girl today writing about "man" in the way I did then. And it isn't that I thought of "man" as someone other than myself. I saw myself included in "man"—in the "man" category—in a way that's hard to credit today.

We are better off, in almost every way, now that literary girls—and boys, for that matter—read women writers. One thing that may sometimes get lost, though, is my presumption that I had a right to write as Martial wrote. I was trying to write with the authority and the gravitas of the men I had read. I had an extraordinary sense of literary entitlement, as a teenager, and great confidence in myself as a writer.

Not having the words to apply to my life at home didn't exactly help, though. It wouldn't be long before I would learn that the confidence I had shown in my earliest writings was built on sand. The tide came in and washed all that away, and it was many years later that I started all over again with my bucket and spade.

The silence at home made it virtually impossible for me to develop into the writer I thought I might become when I was penning epigrams. I had a lot to learn about my father and almost everything to learn about myself before I could properly begin.

In time, though, that silence is also what allowed me to become the writer I am. "When I pronounce the word Silence," the great Polish poet Wisława Szymborska writes, "I destroy it."[12]

There were many reasons to rejoice when I did finally succeed in becoming a writer, but none has been more liberating than finding the words to apply to my youth.

I SHOWED SOME of my work to Mr. Baker, who saw it as Irish. This surprised me; to the extent that I was aware of any influence, I'd have thought of the Latin epigrams I translated in London, but then I was the only one who knew about the translations.

I then handed in an essay as an assignment to my avuncular English teacher, Mr. Irwin. At a very far remove from epigrams, this essay was full of over-wrought emotion and adolescent confusion that had spilled over onto paper, more a cry for help than anything close to good writing. I had been reluctant to show it to Mr. Baker, but I clearly wanted someone to read it. It was never published, mercifully enough, and I have no clear memory of what I said.

With no social circle, no understanding of society, and next to no social life outside the classroom, I was convinced that everything I wrote was private and that no one else would ever know about the piece I handed in to Mr. Irwin. How could I know that teachers compared notes on their students?

NOT EVERY DAY at home was tense, and there were stretches of calm. My sisters and I went on jaunts into the Quebec countryside with Mummy, finding old pine furniture and glass goblets in remote villages. Ian did a lot of reading, and Brian went exploring on the golf course and came back with fossils. In winter, we went tobogganing and took ski classes on the hill stretching down from the clubhouse. Brian went ice-fishing with Daddy, an activity I was happy to avoid. At holiday time, we laughed and danced and whooped it up in the living room.

Sometimes, Mummy drove us all up to Fairview shopping centre, which opened in 1965, and where Granny Jo was delighted to discover the Laura Secord shop. There were no chocolates made by Laura Secord as good as the boxes of Terry's All Gold she had always loved at home, but there were dark chocolates on sale, and she loved the ginger ones best.

School was where I was happiest, though. Mr. Baker occasionally stopped by to chat with our writing group when his day was done, and he started recommending books we might like to read. I had loved *Anne of Green Gables* and was ready for more. My love of reading, then and later, was especially delightful when I found connections with my own life. I loved Louisa May Alcott's *Little Women*, which had been one of Granny Jo's favourites. I read the sequels, as well, taking note of Jo's marriage to the German-sounding Professor Bhaer in *Jo's Boys*. I didn't for a moment suspect that I myself would marry a professor with a German name—or that he and I would have three boys of our own.

Mr. Baker talked about J.D. Salinger, so I read *The Catcher in the Rye*. He talked about Mordecai Richler, who had attended Mr. Baker's own high school in Montreal, Baron Byng—and recommended a novel called *The Apprenticeship of Duddy Kravitz*. I read that, too.

MR. BAKER LISTENED to our little group, as well, but I was used to listening and had rarely been listened to. I had no reason to think anything I might say could be interesting. But Mr. Baker must have been curious about me, because he stopped by our house one evening to meet my parents.

I never learned the reason for this visit, though I did start to wonder about that emotional essay I had handed in to Mr. Irwin, and I was horrified to realize that he must have shown it to Mr. Baker.

Daddy's only comment afterwards was that Mr. Baker was an overgrown schoolboy. Mummy kept her opinion entirely to herself. "Whatever you say, say nothing" had always been her motto, and I didn't press her. Asking questions was risky.

Mr. Baker himself was equally unforthcoming when I next saw him at school. He never said anything to me about that essay, and he made no comment about my parents, either, limiting himself to an amused remark on the marble busts at the front of our house.

The Trojan Women

A new English teacher, John Whitman, set the school abuzz in September 1965, at the start of my graduating year. A small, attractive man with a lively face and floppy dark hair, he had been educated at Yale Drama School. He astonished us all when he announced plans to stage a school production of Euripides's *The Trojan Women*.

It was clear from the outset—from the choice of a Greek tragedy that no one at school had heard of—that this was an ambitious project. Producing an anti-war play was timely, as well, with U.S. ground troops then fighting in Vietnam. The full extent of Mr. Whitman's ambition for the production emerged over the months to come, with each new development more astounding than the last: breathing exercises, voice training, elaborate set and costume design, stark makeup, a choir accompanied by trumpet and percussion, and painstaking choreography for the chorus of twenty pupils drawn from every grade in the school. The mimeographed program, which I still have, names seventy-five teachers and students involved in the production in various capacities, on stage and off.

Ian played Poseidon in the prologue as well as appearing as one of the shield-carrying soldiers later in the play. Brian, who was in Grade 8, played Hector and Andromache's son Astyanax, who gets thrown over the city walls to ensure he will never be able to avenge his father's death.

I coveted the role of Hector's mother, Hecuba—by far the biggest part—and was chagrined when that went to a classmate. Mr. Whitman and the vice-principal sought to mollify me by explaining the strength of the smaller but admittedly more dramatic role they wanted me to play as Andromache. That was a better part for me, they insisted, and they were persuasive. Hecuba's was a mournful role, all wailing and woe, where Andromache was younger and more energetic, a force of nature enraged by the Trojans' defeat, the death of Hector, the murder of her son, and the women's enslavement.

Deeply repressed as I was, it was in playing Andromache that I discovered that I had powerful emotions. On stage, I was expected to express outrage and fury, fear and disgust and love—none of which I had ever dared to express before. The character of Andromache was my shield and my excuse.

And I discovered that I relished the limelight. I had loved playing Oberon at Camden School for Girls, and I loved playing Andromache. There was more, too, for *The Trojan Women* opened my eyes to the possibilities of collaboration on an artistic production.

THE SCHOOL HAD permission to use a church hall in Beacon Hill, north of the school, for rehearsals. Ian, who had his driving licence by this time, used to drive Brian and me over, and, from early November on, the whole gang of us—more than thirty students, Mr. Whitman, and a couple of other teachers drawn by the excitement of the big production—spent every weekend in that church hall.

So my parents spent quieter weekends than usual. There was an unexpected side effect of all the time my brothers and I spent away from the house that winter, too: fewer rows with my father.

Mummy and I shared moments of intimacy, too. I'd been reading *Gaudy Night*, and we talked about Dorothy L. Sayers and her Peter Wimsey books. We talked about Doris Lessing, too, and I was interested to hear Mummy's reasons for admiring her work.

I had one Bob Dylan record, and one by Joan Baez, which I played over and over again in the living room, transcribing the lyrics to their songs.

Mummy came in to listen with me.

"I love Joan Baez's voice," I told her.

We listened to her album, and then I put on Bob Dylan's. I was curious how Mummy would respond to him, for his voice was rough and plaintive—unlike that of any other singer I'd heard.

Mummy surprised me. "His voice is much more interesting than hers," she said.

I listened to Bob Dylan even more intently after that, deciding that Mummy was right about him.

THOSE OF US with starring roles spent most of our weekends hanging around, waiting our turn, while Mr. Whitman rehearsed scenes with other cast members. I had been observing his work with the chorus and started taking over from him when he was busy with another scene. He watched me for a bit, complimented me, and made me production assistant.

I was spending so much time on the production anyway, so why not pitch in? That's the way I thought of it. I loved being one of the stars of the show, but being a star is not a full-time occupation. Instead of hanging around until it was my turn, I wanted to be up and doing.

There was no conflict between being Andromache and being production assistant. Working with the chorus was fun. It was companionable, for I liked working with the other kids and with Mr. Whitman. It was easy for me, too, and it felt natural, for I had developed a few leadership skills in the quasi-parental role I played at home. I was thrilled to be working as production assistant, with the result that *The Trojan Women* revealed not only my talent as an actor but the effectiveness of some of my other skills in the service of a remarkable production.

And it was remarkable. The play ran for three nights, attracting the attention of the *Montreal Star*'s theatre reviewer, which never happened with a school production. My parents sat in the front row during every performance. They were so impressed and so proud of us all that they invited one of Daddy's colleagues and his wife to see the last night of the production, and then served champagne when we all got back to Golf Avenue.

THE SCHOOL YEAR was drawing to an end, and I had just got home from writing the English composition exam. With relations between my father and me steadier, since the play, he asked me how it had gone.

"We had a choice of questions to write on," I told him. He and I were not in the habit of having ordinary conversations. "We were given five different quotations and had to choose one to write about."

"What kind of quotations?"

I pulled the exam questions out of my schoolbag and gave them to him.

Bad idea.

"Which one did you write about?" he asked, warier than he had been when he had first spoken.

I hesitated. I could pretend I'd written on a different quotation, but he'd know, of course. He'd know which one I'd chosen, as he'd have made the same choice.

This was awkward.

"I wrote about the Oscar Wilde quotation," I said, as gamely as I could. Desmond was a great admirer of Wilde's wit.

My father looked stricken.

"It's from *The Picture of Dorian Gray*," I added, but he already knew that. I was playing for time.

The quotation was, "Children begin by loving their parents; as they grow older they judge them; sometimes they forgive them."

That sure put a damper on the conversation.

And what had that quotation inspired me to write? I could see Daddy wondering that.

I wonder that, too. The quotation spoke to me and my own adolescent experience, but I have no idea what I wrote on the examination paper.

I was sorry I'd inadvertently put an end to our conversation.

Sorry, not sorry. I wasn't ready for a serious conversation with Desmond. Not then, not ever.

3. The Napoleonic Wars

IT WAS POSSIBLE by this time for a bright student to find the means to attend university without recourse to the well-to-do relatives required in my parents' day. There was no question that Ian and I—all of us, in due course—were destined for university.

The consensus on women's place in society had advanced since Nan was a student, but not by much. Betty Friedan's *The Feminine Mystique* had been published in 1963, but the influence of the feminist movement, which was drifting north, like an unpredictable weather system, had not yet hit Pointe-Claire.

My own thinking was international, and I had had every hope of winning a scholarship to attend any university I fancied. It was with that in mind that I had tried for the Avon scholarship, which would have given me the wherewithal to go anywhere, but my father had made sure that wouldn't happen. The 1966 Avon scholarship went to a fellow student at BHS.

Desmond thought I should become a secretary. He had great admiration for his own secretary and viewed her job as the pinnacle of professional success, for a woman. When I graduated with the highest grades in the school, he adjusted his plans for me and suggested I become an interpreter.

I was good at languages, but the idea of being an interpreter didn't appeal to me. I was bursting with drive, dying to learn, to start living. I had no interest in marriage, none in children. I wanted so much more than that, and I knew I'd get more.

I also knew enough to keep all this to myself.

NAN LOOKED AFTER herself impeccably, as Granny Jo had always done. There may be a gene that governs shopping behaviour; either that, or the stories Granny Jo had always told about buying herself a new hat every week at Anderson McAuley's in Belfast had merely inspired my mother.

Nan sped up to Fairview with Mandy every Thursday to shop. Driving her new, powder-blue Pontiac Parisienne convertible with the top down, she wore a matching powder-blue chiffon scarf to keep her hair from getting blown around. The new fashions went on display on Thursday morning, and every week she bought herself a new miniskirt, a new sundress, or new shoes. Fortunately, Desmond was earning enough to cover the cost of Nan's extravagances.

She had her hair set and her nails polished at Beaconsfield Shopping Centre, where they told her she looked just like Shirley MacLaine. She had a remarkably solid twenty-year marriage that had survived both ups and downs. She was a sophisticated woman raising five bright and capable children. She was a knowledgeable antique collector with a new specialization in Canadiana, and she had developed a friendly network of collectors and dealers in and around Montreal. She had also been reading articles about women's increasingly multi-dimensional lives—one was headlined "4-D Women"—and she saw herself, as we all saw her, as much more than a housewife.

THE SCHOOL GUIDANCE counsellor, who conducted a standardized test on graduating students, handed me a leaflet with a long list of career possibilities, none of which interested me. Unsurprisingly, as he didn't know me, he failed to offer any guidance. I had loved acting, but my parents did everything to dissuade me from becoming an actor.

Excitable Mr. Whitman cornered me in the hall one afternoon and said, "You have to go to Yale!" He gesticulated with his arms. "You have to! You have to! You have to!"

He knew about the National Theatre School, as one of the faculty members there had been involved in costume design for *The Trojan Women*, but he did not suggest I apply there. In any event, I had missed the deadline for applications to Yale and, without a scholarship, there was no way I could afford to go.

Mr. Baker overheard this exchange, though he didn't say anything at the time. Later that week, he wrapped up a conversation by saying, "And that's why you should study philosophy." We hadn't been talking about what I would do after graduation, and I wasn't sure I'd heard him right, but when I did go to McGill, I enrolled in the honours program in philosophy.

IAN AND I both went on to Grade 12 at Lindsay Place High School, a few miles east of BHS. This was an option of interest mostly to students planning to attend university outside Quebec, as Ian was. Most students who went on to a Quebec university did so directly from Grade 11, and I had an acceptance from McGill. Unlike McGill, though, Grade 12 was free, and that pleased Desmond.

I had been granted a university scholarship at McGill and could cover other expenses out of summer earnings, so Desmond's satisfaction had nothing to do with saving money. He had never had to spend money on my education, and he never would. What he liked best about Grade 12 was that it meant I would stay close to home.

I deferred my scholarship and postponed going to McGill for a year.

WHILE I WAS in Grade 12, I paid a visit to Mr. Baker at BHS, which is where I met another former student on a similar mission, Robin Porter. Mr. Baker had taught him a few years earlier, and Robin's family had immigrated from the UK a few years before mine. He was soon my first boyfriend and a much-needed confidant.

With Robin, who was now at McGill studying Chinese history and Mandarin, I was able for the first time to talk about the experience I'd been living through at home and to see Desmond's behaviour through someone else's eyes. My relationship with Robin was not destined to last, but he was very good to me—and for me—during the two years we were together.

There were academic benefits of going to Grade 12, too. One was that a fierce middle-aged woman named Dr. Alanna Reid Smith taught Canadian history. A scary figure with a bright red face, spiky grey eyebrows, and a wild head of iron-grey hair, Dr. Smith was so knowledgeable about her subject and so excited about the material—and especially the seigneurial system in New France, which had been the subject of her doctoral dissertation at McGill—that she fired me with enthusiasm about Canada. This was no mean feat, given Desmond's derisive attitude to everything Canadian. I was never close to the assertively intellectual Dr. Smith, but she left me with a lifelong respect both for bluestockings and for Canada.

The other unexpectedly good result of going to Grade 12 was that I came under the influence of René Laine, a French teacher from France who had been permitted to teach us because he happened to be from a Protestant family. Such were the times, in the depths of the English-speaking West Island of Montreal in 1966, that his name was pronounced as if it were the English name "Lane," rather than the French name "Laine," which rhymes with "pen." And such were the times that he didn't bother to correct us.

Monsieur Laine, who was not only engaging, but also literary, is the reason I chose to continue studying French when I went on to McGill in 1967. And it was in French class at McGill that I read Benjamin Constant's *Adolphe* and found my vocation.

4.
Fugitive

The writers you read
when young seem not only
close to you, but prophetic.
—MAVIS GALLANT, interview,
Canadian Fiction Magazine

The Salonnière

I have fallen in love many times, mostly with books. Translating Latin poetry was my first love, as a twelve-year-old in London, and I was seventeen when I read *Adolphe*.

Adolphe introduced me to romance. The perfect book to read at the start of a literary career, it may be essential reading for a young woman on the brink of life.

The author, Benjamin Constant, was a French writer whose family had settled in Lausanne and who became one of the most highly regarded intellectuals of the early nineteenth century. He met Germaine de Staël in 1794, they fell in love, and *Adolphe* was in part inspired by their affair, which ended years before his novel was published in 1816.

Constant's is a man's view of romance, but when I read *Adolphe* in 1967, I had not yet discovered it was possible to read books from a woman's point of view— or that there is such a thing as a woman's point of view. In falling for the novel, I was thrilled by what Constant wrote about Ellénore, the young Polish woman Adolphe falls in love with, and I was dazzled by his rapturous account of Ellénore's intelligence, her cosmopolitanism, her liberal ideas, and her daring.

What struck me, at the age of seventeen, was not only Adolphe's love for Ellénore, although that seemed the epitome of love. What struck me especially was the *way* Constant writes about Adolphe's love for Ellénore.

Ellénore speaks several languages imperfectly, he says, but she speaks them in a lively way and sometimes with grace. She seems to struggle to express her ideas, and he is smitten.

> *Elle parlait plusieurs langues, imparfaitement à la vérité, mais toujours avec vivacité, quelque-fois avec grâce. Ses idées semblaient se faire jour à travers les obstacles, et sortir de cette lutte plus agréables, plus naïves et plus neuves ; car les idiomes étrangers rajeunissent les pensées, et les débarrassent de ces tournures qui les font paraître tour à tour communes et affectées.*

> She spoke several languages, in actual fact not perfectly, but always with vivacity and sometimes with elegance. Her ideas seemed to come out from behind a barrier, and to emerge from this struggle more attrac-tive, more naïve and fresher; for foreign languages rejuvenate ideas and strip them of those expressions which make them appear, in turn, either commonplace or affected.[13]

I loved that. I wanted someone to say something like that about me. Not right then, necessarily. Enthralled by literature and philosophy, I wanted to be a woman about whom that could be said. I would lead my life with these words in mind.

I spoke French very imperfectly, far more imperfectly than Ellénore, and neither vivaciously nor gracefully. I did not speak several languages, having long ago forgotten German and the Basler dialect. Though I'd never spoken Latin, I had been able to read it, and was now in the process of forgetting that, as well.

It is this passage in *Adolphe* that persuaded me to enroll in a German language course at McGill. With its textbook exercises and language labs, however, German at McGill was impossibly far from the world in which I had spoken German in Basel. What that course taught me was how little I remembered of a language I once knew at least as well as I knew English.

I ESPECIALLY LOVED the evocative words *"car les idiomes étrangers rajeunissent les pensées,"* which epitomize the beauty of French, expressing as they do a substantial idea—about language, about expressions in a foreign language, and about the effect of such expressions on thought—with such economy and felicity that I never forgot them.

Constant's words touched on everything that mattered to me. I couldn't pretend that they applied to my romantic seventeen-year-old self, but I was thinking ahead. Somehow, I would live up to these words.

Constant's comments on Ellénore's use of language introduced another new idea. If foreign idioms can enliven our thinking, I should be seeking out speakers of foreign languages. However foreign a language might be, it can make it possible to think in new ways.

There was more, too, and I didn't hesitate to apply the lessons of this paragraph to my own life. I had struggled with bewilderment ever since I was a small child, starting with that first journey across the Irish Sea—a bewilderment with the ever-changing circumstances in which I found myself.

Bewilderment was associated with displacement. It was associated with a simple failure to understand the words that supposedly applied to particular circumstances. Sometimes this was because the words were in a foreign language, but I was often bewildered in English, too. Latin had seemed easier, but no one I knew actually spoke Latin. Perhaps it seemed easier because no one I knew actually spoke Latin.

This sense of bewilderment was my natural element. It did seem to me that other people struggled less than I did. Some people felt at home—*were* at home. Some people had never left the one place they knew. I envied them the ease and clarity they seemed to enjoy, and wondered if I myself would ever emerge into a clearing.

And now, here was Adolphe describing Ellénore's ideas as emerging *through* obstacles—and as being all the better for that.

Could there be something of value about the struggle itself?

This was going to require a rethink.

So, that one rich paragraph not only fired me with enthusiasm for foreign languages and the company of strangers, it also opened up the possibility of viewing my own struggle to express myself in a new light.

ADOLPHE AND ELLÉNORE read the English poets together, they took long walks together, and they talked about a thousand things. He often went to see her in the morning, returning in the evening.

I was a novice at literary criticism and had certainly not thought of conversation as a genre that could be appreciated as a poem might be, or analyzed as I was now learning to analyze a Socratic dialogue.

That's part of what Adolphe is doing with Ellénore. He is not only her lover; he is her adoring literary critic, paying close attention to every word she utters. His love for her is inextricably linked to his love of what she says and the idiosyncratic ways in which she says it. Nothing could be more romantic, I decided, choosing to ignore Ellénore's unhappy eventual fate.

I WAS INTRIGUED, too, by the little I knew about Germaine de Staël. Her father was a Swiss banker who had been director-general of finance under Louis XIV, and her mother hosted a literary salon in Paris. As a girl, Germaine had dazzled salon guests, and by the time she married a Swedish diplomat in 1786, when she was twenty, she had published plays and essays and was one of the leading figures of her day.

One of her novels, *Corinne, or Italy*,[14] outsold the works of Walter Scott, and she was celebrated both as a writer and as a liberal intellectual. I did not go to the lengths of reading her work when I was at McGill; it was *Adolphe* that inspired me, and it was what I knew about Staël's life that fascinated me. The mother of four children, she herself became a *salonnière*, famous for hosting not only Constant, but Wilhelm Schlegel, Friedrich von Schiller, the Comte de Narbonne, Lord Byron, and dozens of other European writers, artists, and intellectuals in Paris and at her Swiss estate, and was "the most outstanding, innovative, and notorious woman writer of her age."[15]

A true European, and highly political, she acted as a kind of unofficial opposition to Napoleon Bonaparte. Her views—and her forthright manner, which he disliked in a woman—irritated him to such an extent that he banished her three times between 1803 and 1812.

I could never lead the kind of life Staël led. I would never have the kinds of advantages she had, for a start. It was Staël's wealth and her position that provided her opportunities—and helped protect her from the harm society inflicts on a woman who dares to flout convention.

I didn't have her history of stunning the intelligentsia, either, or her circle of gifted friends, lovers, and fellow exiles. I was a shy young woman on the cusp of a life in an altogether different world, and I was dreaming way above my station.

The idea I had of Madame de Staël was like a cameo, showing her profile and revealing little of the real woman who walked this earth. The cameo is not a true likeness; it's imprecise and barely recognizable, but no less appealing for all that. Perhaps all the more appealing, because of that. I had fallen for the vaguest outline of an independent life for an intellectual woman.

STAËL'S EXPERIENCE AS a *salonnière* was one thing that appealed to me. I loved the idea of gathering talented people together to talk about books and theatre, art and politics and ideas. There would be pale wines in pretty glasses and dainty morsels to eat. There would be walls hung with paintings and tapestries, and magnif-icent gardens with marble statues, fountains, poplars, weeping willows, flowering shrubs. I pictured myself wearing beautiful clothes and fanciful hats, like a character in a *fête galante*.

It would help to be rich, and I knew I would never be rich, not only because I lacked a wealthy family, but also because I had inherited a Bolshevik disdain for riches. If I were to dig for gold, it would be literary gold.

I was dimly aware that there were people whose goal in life was to make lots of money, but I didn't know anyone like that, and I wholeheartedly disapproved of them. What possible reason could there be to devote your life to the quest for money? If that really was your goal, I was sure you must be leading a very dull and conventional life—and wasting your time on work so boring that it could inspire no nobler purpose.

I wanted work that would thrill me. I wanted to live a bohemian life. And not any old bohemian life, either. I wanted to be surrounded by foreigners, by writers, artists, intellectuals. And I wanted a life that would work for a woman. For me.

If I were ever to know accomplished men and women, and if I were ever to host elegant *soirées*, it would surely help to be sociable, too. I was tongue-tied and ill at ease socially.

I myself would need to be a pretty accomplished woman, I knew. I'd have to be bright, and I knew I was bright. I'd have to speak French and another language or two; I could work on that. I'd have to be a writer, too. And why not? That was part of the dream. I had been writing for several years already, and some of what I'd written had even appeared in print.

I had other advantages. Uprootedness, anxiety, secrets, a passion for translation, a curiosity about writers, an interest in the wider world, and a good education. I had a social conscience, too—in large part thanks to Desmond's Sunday evening sermons—and a desire to make the world a better place. I had a good dose of Celtic indignation, also thanks to my father, a taste for revolution, and a lot more ambition than anyone thought seemly in a woman, then or now.

These don't all look like advantages, or not all the time. The benefits of uprootedness are evident only to a person with a sturdy constitution and plenty of support, and there have been times I had neither. Anxiety has caused me such grief that it's a stretch to consider it an advantage; I do so because it has also inspired me to act in ways I would not otherwise have acted—and to persist long after less anxious souls would have sensibly given up. Secrets are a mixed blessing, too, enriching my imaginative life, if not my social skills.

There were times when I lost sight of this dream. I never forgot it, though, even when I had to bide my time.

"*Salonnière*" IS ITSELF a romantic word, with an old-fashioned French lustre. I had never come across the word in a book, and I never heard it used—and certainly not in any discussion of what I would do with my life. Not in discussions with the guidance counsellor, not in conversations with Mr. Whitman and Mr. Baker. No one ever told me what the word means, probably because there was no one I had ever met—except, no doubt, M. Laine—who so much as knew the word. By the time I was seventeen, though, I knew that's what I wanted to be. I wanted more than that, too, but I definitely wanted that. My future was written in those distant stars.

It would take a long time for me to become a *salon-nière*, and when I did, I was slow to realize that was what had happened. I was persistent, though, and I worked hard. I gritted my teeth, more than once, and did what had to be done.

Does that sound grim? There have been tough times. My nature is optimistic, though. There has been fun, too, love, pleasure, adventure, delight. And what I was doing, almost always, was exactly what I wanted to be doing. I am a fortunate woman.

I had a few talents, nowhere near enough, but over time I developed other talents, too, as you do, as you have to. It took a long time before I learned how to stop my voice shaking when making a telephone call. I was timid when out of my element, which was so much of the time, but I did eventually learn how to present myself at a meeting with confidence, or at least—there are times those acting skills have come in handy—the appearance of confidence. I developed an ability to persuade, occasionally to inspire. I discovered how to look as though I'm at ease at a cocktail party, a reception, a festival opening, even when I would give anything to be at home, on my own.

I have been rewarded by some success, more than anyone expected. And always, in every venture, it has been the dream that sustained me. Long before I knew how to make a literary life happen, I knew this was the life for me.

I WAS WRONG about one thing, for I was drawn to Paris and was sure that was where I would find this enticing future. Not in a leafy suburb of Montreal, no. Not in

Northern Ireland, which rarely crossed my mind. Not in Basel, which had vanished from memory. Not in London, either. That was in the past, and I was facing the future. All that was real, and I was dreaming.

I did go to Paris, soon enough, but I was wrong to think I could leave behind everything I'd ever known.

Les Fleurs du mal

dolphe is not the only French book that inspired me during my first semester at McGill. My copy of *Les Fleurs du mal* still has my name inside, in the script I used that year and never again. Linda Leith, with an *e* like an epsilon—we literary types have our affectations—and the date of purchase, *Sept. 30, 1967*. The word *"Les"* is top right, with *"Fleurs du mal"* immediately underneath, flush right.

I open my age-softened copy today with a new interest, for I am now a publisher, and I have a professional interest in a book published by the legendary French house Larousse. Bottom right is the company logo, a prettily decorated capital letter *L*. Inside the *L* is the tiny image of a girl holding a stem between the thumb and index finger of her right hand. The image is so small that it looks like a lit sparkler, but this is the stem of a windblown dandelion. Half-encircling the girl and the dandelion seeds are the words *"Je sème à tout vent"*—I sow to all winds.

I didn't notice the publisher's affectations in 1967, and my interest was in the dark photograph of Charles Baudelaire (*Phot. Carjat*) and the title page opposite. The page is busy with information about the founder (*Félix Guirand, Agrégé des Lettres*) and director (*Léon Lejealle, Agrégé des Lettres*) of Classiques Larousse, and the poet's surname—no Charles this time, just Baude-laire—over the title: LES FLEURS DU MAL, followed by *choix de poèmes*.

A list follows of biographical, historical, and explan-atory notes included in this slim volume of 110 pages—as well as commentary, a questionnaire, and homework topics prepared by Adrien Cart (*Agrégé des Lettres*) and Mlle S. Hamel (*Licenciée ès Lettres*).

No fewer than four individuals have their full names and academic credentials on the title page, in other words, where the poet himself gets just his surname. A further note informs the reader this is a new edition, and the page ends with the addresses of three Larousse book-stores in Paris VI: at 17, rue du Montparnasse; at boule-vard Raspail, 114; and at 58, rue des Écoles (Sorbonne).

These pages conjured up a whole new realm in my imagination. This slim volume was academically sound and destined for the educational market. I understood, too, that there must be glory in being identified by a single name—Baudelaire. And indeed there is, as Bono and Beyoncé remind us.

And I pored over the poems. The book is now so fragile that I turn the pages gently. I read "L'Invitation au voyage," a poem addressed to *"mon enfant, ma sœur"* as a personal invitation *"d'aller là-bas vivre ensemble !"*

> *Aller là-bas*? Go over there?
> But where?

What's over there?

Là, tout n'est qu'ordre et beauté,
Luxe, calme et volupté.

Volupté. What a word! Desmond's "Mirror calm"
was good. Epigrams were models of concision. But *luxe,
calme et volupté*! This was an enticing sensual ideal. A
utopia.

I couldn't wait.

THERE ARE DETAILED notes beside dozens of the
poems—my handwritten notes about *l'art pour l'art,*
about religious symbols, about allusions to the poet's
love for Madame Sabatier. There are questions I jotted
down in French in the margins—*pourquoi l'Horreur
est un des bijoux de la Beauté?*—and translations into
English of words new to me—*archer, la nuée, bâillement,
anacoluthe, glapissants.*

Beside the poem "Bénédiction," I underlined the word
"*Poete*" and wrote that Baudelaire's insistence on writing
the word in this way (rather than as "*poète*") was an
affectation.

These were some of the greatest love poems I would
ever read, in any language, and I was entranced. By the
time I'd read Baudelaire, I was in love with love.

And I never again dared to imagine I could write in
French.

WHAT I DIDN'T like was the image of Baudelaire
himself. He looks ill and wretched in that sombre photograph, and if there is passion in his face, it's closer to

anger than to love. He was the raison d'être of all the work that had gone into the book, but I found him repellent. I did want to be part of the world this book conjured up, the world of writers and books, of literature and love, but it was impossible to want to be like Baudelaire, no matter how great a poet he was. No amount of glory was worth that much misery.

I did give Mlle S. Hamel some thought. Though a lesser figure than the others named on the title page, she was the only one I felt any connection to. This was because she was a woman, where there was something forbidding about all the men, and I had had enough of forbidding men.

It wasn't that I wanted to be like Mademoiselle Hamel, but I would have liked to know more about her. She had devoted time and energy to putting material together for students of the poems. I approved of that. Mademoiselle Hamel was part of that literary world, too, and I envied her that. But what was she like? I had no way of knowing.

What I wanted was a way into the world Mademoiselle Hamel was a part of. I could imagine no role for myself there, but what I wanted, more than anything, was to walk along rue du Montparnasse, boulevard Raspail, and rue des Écoles.

So that's what I did. It took me another three years, but that is where I headed as soon as I could.

IN THE MEANTIME, I still had to leave home.

With the help of a friend of Robin's, I was hired for the summer at the Manoir Richelieu. This is a resort hotel in what was once known as Murray Bay—now Saint-Étienne de La Malbaie—on the north shore of the Saint

Lawrence east of Quebec City. I worked as assistant to the storekeeper and enjoyed the pool, the tennis courts, and the company of other students in the off hours, for the hotel was staffed to a large extent by students.

When I returned to Montreal in August, Robin had rented an apartment in the student ghetto east of McGill. This was an inspiration, and when I myself found a studio apartment across the street from Robin, I rented it and moved in.

Nan and Desmond were shocked, and I was disowned. You were either a full, enthusiastic member of the Leith family, or you were out on your ear. In neither case was there anything to discuss, though there were a couple of stormy scenes and the inevitable silences.

I was not the first to leave. Granny Jo had long gone by this time and was back in Northern Ireland. Ian had been living in residence at Trent University in Peterborough, Ontario. My departure was different, though, for my parents knew that my decision to move out was a protest.

The impact of this protest was greatly lessened when my mother developed a debilitating back problem that fall, and I started commuting back to Pointe-Claire every weekend to help keep the household running.

The point had been made, nonetheless. Leaving home marked a new era in my relations with my parents. Though there were difficulties ahead, I was never again treated as badly as I had been before I escaped.

IT WAS AT the Manoir that I met Andy Gollner. A Hungarian refugee and a student of political science at Loyola College in Montreal—this was before Loyola joined with Sir George Williams to form Concordia

University in 1974—he was working as the hotel paymaster. The accounting office was in the "maids and chauffeurs" wing of the hotel, across the hall from the room I shared with another staffer. I took an interest in Andy, he took an interest in me, and he took me along to meet some Hungarian friends in Quebec City one evening. He called me in Montreal that fall, too, to invite me to a party, but I was with Robin.

Andy was there again the following summer. My room was now in the staff house, behind the hotel, for the storekeeper had behaved inappropriately with me at the end of my first summer, and I'd chosen to be one of the waitresses in the vast dining room, serving the private guests whose numbers were dwindling—as well as conventions of grocers from all over Quebec and sundry gatherings from other industries.

I saw Andy when he came into the kitchen for his breakfast, and sometimes we headed down the hill to Castel's—the English-speaking staff's name for the local bar, Castel de la mer—with a bunch of others for a drink and dancing after work. He was five years older than I—a big age difference when you're eighteen—and a good dancer. I thought him debonair and fun, and I fell in love.

Gollner, more properly Göllner, sounded German, though Andy had been born in Budapest at the end of the war and had lived in Hungary until the 1956 revolution. I wasn't sure what to make of the fact that he was Hungarian, although this was certainly part of his appeal. I had loved *My Fair Lady* and the Prince of Transylvania, though less taken by Zoltan Karpathy. Did I remember the refugee centre in Basel? Not consciously. I do remember being startled when Andy's mother called from Montreal to chat with Andy. That was the first time

I heard Hungarian spoken, and it sounded impossibly foreign. His name was András, I learned, though he has always been Andy to me.

We started heading down to Castel's without a gang, just the two of us, and he walked me back up the hill to the Manoir at the end of these evenings. We got to the door of my room, where he looked at me and shook my hand. The same thing happened the next time, and the time after that. After three weeks of this, I looked at him quizzically, wondering why he didn't kiss me. And then he did.

Paris

In 1970, Desmond was appointed medical director of Pfizer Europe, so my way was paid when the whole Leith family left for Brussels that June, shortly after my graduation from McGill. From Brussels, it was an easy train ride to Paris, and that's where I wanted to be. I'd been dying to get back to Europe, and this was too good an opportunity to miss. Andy and I agreed to write during the months we'd be apart.

I spent the summer plotting. My parents had rented a house in the Flemish commune of Overijse, and I helped with the move and the settling in, discovering that French was worse than useless in a Flemish community. Suburban Overijse was hardly the Europe I had dreamed of, but it was a giant step in the right direction. I explored Brussels and sipped *café filtre* in the Grand Place with Ian and Brian. I reread Auden's poem "Musée des Beaux Arts" and sought out the museum and the Bruegel image of Daedalus falling out of the sky.

Ian and I read a history of the Battle of Waterloo and drove over to the battlefield to study the landscape and trace the progress of Napoleon's last stand. Brian and I walked down the hill from our house to the francophone lakeside community of Genval for beer and commiseration about the sweethearts we had left behind in Canada.

So, I drifted through the summer, sure only of what I would do next, which was to enroll in a course in French civilization at the Sorbonne. I would find a cheap place to live—I had a little money left—and I would write poetry and start leading that bohemian life I had dreamed of.

IT WAS EARLY September when I stepped off a train in the Gare du Nord, and I soon found lodgings in an attic room in a building on rue Joseph-Bara, partway between rue du Montparnasse and boulevard Raspail, and up the road from rue des Écoles. I would live rent-free in return for English conversation with the owners' adolescent daughter, Marie-Pierre. This suited me very well and left me plenty of time to enjoy Paris, go to class, and write.

Marie-Pierre already spoke English passably well, having had a series of tutors before I arrived on the scene, so the conversation went well. Both her parents were corporate lawyers, crisp and correct. My classes, which were held in a vast auditorium, consisted of lectures delivered in a monotone by bored professors. It was far more fun to stroll across the city, visit the Orangerie or the Louvre, and stop off at a café with my notebook. A high school classmate was in Paris that year, as well, and I hung out with him and a new friend, trying out the student cafeteria, going to movies and munching fat Tunisian sandwiches in the Quartier Latin.

I was writing in a café near Port-Royal one evening when two older couples came in and ordered wine. I recognized Samuel Beckett at once, and watched this group for a while, wondering whether I had the nerve to speak to him. He noticed me and must have known I recognized him—it would have happened often, for the Nobel Prize for Literature had catapulted him to fame the previous year. He looked craggy and stern, exactly the way he looked in the photographs I'd seen of him. I was thrilled to see him, and far too shy to approach him. I was certain, too, that he didn't want me to go over and start up a conversation. And what would I have said to him, anyway? That I loved *Endgame*?

It was true. There was no one I admired more than Beckett, and I did admire *Endgame* especially. I had read all E.M. Forster's novels, first *A Passage to India*, then *Howards End* and all the others. I did not love all D.H. Lawrence's work, but *Sons and Lovers* had impressed me, and I thought Lawrence bold and unconventional. Unlike those and the many other writers I read in my English courses at McGill, though, Beckett had fascinated me from the start.

Waiting for Godot, *Happy Days*, and *Endgame* were mysteries I felt compelled to solve, so I read further, spending weeks poring over the thesis on Proust that Beckett wrote as a student at Trinity College Dublin, and delving into the disconcerting novels he had written in English before the success of *Godot*—all this in an attempt to find out where those extraordinary plays had come from.

I spent years focusing a great deal of attention on that very question, and I never regretted that I left him and his companions in peace that evening near Port-Royal.

BACK IN MONTREAL, Andy had been hired as a sessional lecturer in political science at Loyola College and was living in a small apartment on Tupper Street. The separation, the letters, and the phone calls from Brussels were bringing us closer together than ever. He wrote to me in Paris about a song entitled "If You Do Believe in Love" and mailed me a copy of the record. When it arrived in pieces, he mailed me another copy.

I was writing diligently in my garret—journals, notes on books I'd been reading and films I'd seen, long letters to Andy, to my McGill friend Margaret, to Granny Jo— but the poetry was not working out. I produced page after page, read over what I had written, and found it lacking.

I kept at it, but writing is difficult. When you tweak one word, another needs reworking. So, I tweaked this and reworked that, and then copied the whole thing out and read it over again. Still no good.

After the first couple of months, I had many poems in this state of terminal unreadiness. I decided to string them together. That took another month of work, but I couldn't convince myself the result was any improvement. By then it was December.

Living in Paris was everything I had hoped, but the writing was a flop.

Did I tell anyone I was unhappy with my progress? I did not. Did I seek help? No. I had no idea where I might find help and no practice looking for help.

No one else had read a word I wrote that fall, not Margaret, not even Andy, and I trusted my own negative judgment unquestioningly. I knew no one who read poetry except as course work, and no one at all who wrote poetry. I had not brought a single book of poems with me to Paris, not even *Les Fleurs du mal*. I had never been to a poetry reading and didn't even know there was such a thing.

I wasn't interested in contemporary poets and would have had difficulty naming more than one or two. The truth was, I wasn't all that interested in poetry, though I wasn't ready to admit that to myself. Poetry seemed so personal and so private that it didn't occur to me that there was anything I could learn from other poets.

What if I had managed to write a good poem? Would I have known it was any good? Probably not.

And why was I so focused on poetry, when I could have tried writing in other genres?

I had no idea what I was doing.

THERE WERE PRACTICAL considerations, too. I had never heard of writing workshops, which had not existed at McGill, and this was decades before there was a Quebec Writers' Federation offering affordable workshops for aspiring writers. A creative writing program had been set up at Sir George Williams in Montreal, but I doubted the value of such programs and knew nothing about this one. In any event, I couldn't afford tuition fees, and I would never have asked my father for help. His mantra was, "He who pays the piper calls the tune," and I didn't want to play my father's tune.

I was running out of money, fast. I needed to find paid work, and the one thing I did know about poetry is that it would never be lucrative.

I had dreamed of being a writer without any clear idea about what that might mean. I had convinced myself I just needed to hang out in Paris, breathe the literary air, and go for it. When that didn't do the trick, I despaired.

I celebrated my twenty-first birthday in Paris in mid-December, and Andy wrote to let me know he'd been accepted into the PhD program at the London School of Economics. "Come back to Montreal," he wrote. "I'd like you to move in here, and then we can go to London together in September."

THE CRUCIAL TRAITS Andy and I had in common were that we had both been displaced, and we both had dominant fathers. Andy and I came from dissimilar worlds, though, and there were vast differences between us, as well.

His parents had been upper-middle-class Hungarians before the postwar Communist takeover—churchgoing, well-to-do, and politically conservative—where my parents were lifelong socialists from lower-middle-class and working-class families in Northern Ireland.

Where my father had been a country doctor and was now a corporate executive, Andy's father, also András but known as Bandi, was an agronomist trained at the University of Debrecen who had been assigned to manage a collective farm near the Austrian border in the years leading up to 1956. His work took him out on the land, while Edit, his wife, lived in a small village with their two daughters and Andy, who was the youngest. A tall, handsome man, Bandi rode back to the village on horseback, and promptly beat Andy for whatever mischief he had been up to that week.

Sympathetic to the farmers whose land had been confiscated to create the collective farms, Bandi knew he had no future in Hungary after the Communist Party overseer had him declared an enemy of the people. When the Russian tanks rolled into Budapest in 1956 to put down the uprising, Bandi decided it was time to flee. A friendly farmer drove the family close to the border, and then Bandi led them into Austria on foot. The farmer was later arrested for helping them escape.

After a few months in a camp for displaced persons in Austria, Canada took them in and sent them to a refugee camp in rural Quebec. When Bandi was hired by Macdonald College, McGill's agricultural college, they all moved to Sainte-Anne-de-Bellevue, on the western tip of the island of Montreal.

Knowing no language other than Hungarian, Bandi rode the campus garbage truck, at first, which was a terrible comedown. Once he had learned English, he became manager of the experimental farm, but he declined the teaching position he was offered, thinking his English was not good enough for that. He never attained the status he had had in his own country, and Andy never stopped being haunted by the image of him on horseback.

Being refugees was an ordeal, in other words. In order to make it all worthwhile, Andy was supposed to make good, and to make good along lines his parents approved of. That meant medicine, ideally, though dentistry and engineering would also have been acceptable. Political science didn't cut it, especially since Andy's political views were developing in directions that scandalized his parents.

ANDY WAS NEVER close to Nan and Desmond, who treated him poorly, but he did find their unconventionality and their politics appealing. Edit and Bandi were always good to me, and I loved them. As part of

146

a nuclear family that had bounced around in an isolation chamber, I found their huge extended family enormously appealing.

Where my childhood summers had been spent in Belfast, Basel, or London, Andy had spent his in a small village north of Budapest. There, he spent months surrounded by orchards, tennis courts, and fields of sunflowers in the company not only of his parents and sisters but also of almost twenty cousins, his grandparents, and a dozen or more aunts, uncles, and family friends. It sounded gorgeous.

I also loved the Hungarian language, with its assertive consonants and its mystery, and I'd been doing my best to learn a few words and phrases. Edit was a wonderful cook, and I relished her *karfiolleves*, and her *pörkölt*, and her hazelnut torte—practically all Hungarian food.

I read and reread Andy's letter, longing to see him again. I had thought there was something romantic about being alone in Paris—that a writer needs to be alone. When I stopped getting my mail after a misunderstanding with the concierge, I felt cut off and lonely.

ANDY CALLED WHILE I was in Brussels for Christmas, and we made our plans. He was saving his pennies, for his acceptance from the LSE did not include funding. I could barely put together enough money to cover my airfare back to Montreal, but I would be able to work and save up some money of my own once I got there.

I returned to Paris with little more than a month to go before my Sorbonne course ended. Then I bounded onto a plane to Montreal—which was then rerouted to New York. For some reason, I wasn't allowed off the plane in Montreal, which was frustrating. Not having planned to travel to New York, there was a further delay at LaGuardia because I had no U.S. visa.

So, it took me many hours to get back to Montreal. Having had no way of reaching Andy to let him know what was happening, I expected I'd have to make my own way downtown, and I was overjoyed to see him at the arrivals gate. He had been waiting all that time.

It was the start of an idyll.

MY TYPING SKILLS guaranteed me an undemanding, uninteresting, and ill-paid job, and I was hired by Honeywell, where I impressed my boss without making any effort to do so. Computer companies were recruiting talent for a growing industry, and he offered to enroll me in a training course. Computing skills would have provided a better income than typing, in the years before I found my feet (and quite likely thereafter, as well), but I didn't take the offer seriously. The boss had his eye on my body, and I couldn't wait to get out of there.

Andy and I moved from Tupper Street to an apartment on Pine Avenue that Margaret, finishing up her MA at McGill, had been sharing with other students.

Then, in July, Nan called.

This never happened.

"Desmond has had a breakdown," she told me. I still didn't know about his hospitalization in 1954.

There must be more to follow. Nan would not be calling if there weren't more to follow.

"He's on medical leave," Nan went on, then paused.

I waited.

"The reason I'm calling," she now said, "is to let you know that Pfizer is transferring Desmond from Europe to East Africa at the end of the summer. To Nairobi."

I had no rejoinder to this, no thought of a rejoinder.
Nairobi.

I did have a sense of dread.

"This is a big move," Nan added, "and it's important to keep the family together."

I took a deep breath. The air in the apartment was starting to smell like radiator fluid.

"We'd like you to come with us," she said finally.

"But I'll be in London," I said. "Andy and I are flying to London in September." She had known about our plans ever since I'd been in Brussels for Christmas.

"Yes, I know you said that, but Desmond and I—and all of us—would really like you to come with us."

She wanted me to leave Andy and fly halfway across the world to be with them. It was a terrible moment, but my choice was clear.

I shook my head. "I can't do that, Mummy. I really can't."

I HAD PLANS to meet with a high school friend the next day, and I'm ashamed to say I forgot about her after my mother's call.

There was another call from Brussels, on the following weekend, and this time my father came on the line.

"We want you to come to Nairobi with us," he said. "Everyone else is coming. Ian is coming. Granny Jo. Brian, Sheelagh, Mandy. You should come, too."

His voice was like honey.

I listened, sick at heart. I had defied my parents before, but never over anything of such import. I was afraid that refusing to join them would create a rift that might never heal.

I refused.

They didn't call again, but I knew they hadn't given up.

London, Again

As a Canadian citizen, Andy had no right to work in the UK. I did have that right, for I was still a British subject and could find a job if the need arose. We knew the need would arise. We had both saved what we could, and Andy's parents had given him a further amount, all they could afford, but it was nowhere near enough.

We stayed with the parents of a McGill friend in Pimlico for a couple of weeks until we moved into the attic room of a small row house in Muswell Hill. The academic year began, and Andy set off for the Aldwych and the London School of Economics. My plan, as before, was to write.

Writing was what I wanted to do; I just had to learn how to do it better. I took the first positive step towards becoming a writer when I enrolled in a creative writing course at Morley College, once a working man's college and now an adult education centre.

This was the first time I had shared my work with others since high school, and though I found it humbling to have my work criticized, I was curious to see the work of others and to hear people talk about the process of writing. I had started writing prose, leaving poetry behind. I had a good model, too, as I'd been reading Virginia Woolf's novels, on Margaret's recommendation, and was very impressed.

I began to contemplate an academic career; that looked like a good way to indulge my passion for books.

There were ways of becoming a librarian, if that had been my wish, perhaps even a bookseller, if I got to know the right people. I didn't know how to become an editor, though I liked the idea of editing. But a writer? You make your own road, or you don't.

And you need to know a lot more than I knew, as a young woman. In some cases—my own, certainly— you need to have lived more and understood more. It helps to know yourself better than I then did, and to have developed your own voice. It would be many years before I got to that point.

THERE WAS A well-trodden route to an academic career. This was the path Andy had chosen, and it looked like a good direction for me, too. I applied to the University of London for the MPhil program in English literature. I had read many writers during my undergraduate years at McGill, including most of Dostoevsky's novels. Reading his fiction for myself had given me a new respect for Granny Jo, whose favourite Russian writer he had been.

Granny Jo had called him "Dostovisky," which had seemed amusing at the time. Having heard my parents disparage Northern Irish provincialisms, I'd always thought of "Dostovisky" as a product of Granny Jo's lack of cosmopolitanism, so *The Idiot* taught me a lesson in humility, and not only because Prince Myshkin's Christian humility is at the heart of the novel. It taught me I had underestimated Granny Jo, for I now knew how far ahead of me she had always been. It also taught lessons I needed to learn about what really matters.

When it came to applying for postgraduate work in London, the writer I proposed to work on was Samuel Beckett. I'd left him in peace in that café in Port-Royal, but I was as fascinated by his work as ever. Here was an Irishman who began his writing career unsuccessfully in English, then chose to write in French instead, had a huge impact, and started translating much of his own work into English. I proposed to explore the early fictions he wrote in English as a way into his work.

Andy and I both applied for funding from the government agencies in Ottawa and Quebec City that support graduate studies.

IT WAS LATE October when I next heard from my parents, who were now settled in Nairobi and wanted me to join them for the holidays. I had grave doubts about this, fearing more pressure to stay with them, but I did like the idea of seeing my brothers and sisters, and Granny Jo, who had now left Northern Ireland for good. I cherished some hope of establishing better relations with my parents. The idea of two months in the tropics was appealing, as well, after a wet, dreary autumn in London. Pfizer would pay my way there and back.

Andy, for his part, was contemplating a return visit to Hungary, which he hadn't seen since his family had fled fifteen years earlier. He and I decided to go our separate ways for the holidays.

I SPENT A luxurious time in the house Nan and Desmond had rented on 1st Ngong Avenue. Congo, a man in his fifties who was referred to as the "houseboy," looked after the domestic chores, including the cooking. There was a gardener, too; that's how executives working for multinational corporations lived in Nairobi. With no kitchen duties and no babies to look after, I was free to lead a life of leisure.

My parents were determined to please me. After Christmas, they drove the three of us through Tsavo National Park, where Desmond went out of his way to provoke an angry elephant, to Mombasa. From that perfumed city on the Indian Ocean, we headed up the coast and spent a few days in Malindi, where I went snorkelling in the coral reef. When we got back to Nairobi, Nan bought me a spectacular cotton skirt in deep Kenyan colours.

It was too good to be true, of course. By the end of January, they were pressuring me to stay.

ANDY WAS BACK in London by this time, having spent an intense and emotionally charged time in Budapest. He sent telegrams and then called at unthinkable expense when he heard about my parents' efforts to get me to stay in Nairobi. I told them I wanted to return to London, to be with Andy, and then I told them again. And again.

I'd refused them before, when they'd called me in Montreal the previous summer, but Andy had been with me then. He was now a world away, and they were doing everything in their power to convince me to stay.

What were they thinking? There was no life for me in Nairobi.

And what if I had agreed? I had about ten pounds to my name. I had no legal right to work in Kenya, so there was no possibility of my earning a living there. Staying in Nairobi would have been the end of my relationship with Andy. It would have been the end of everything I was and everything I wanted to be.

I was reminded of the savage ending of Evelyn Waugh's *A Handful of Dust*, in which the protagonist, Tony Last, makes it to a legendary city in the Amazonian rainforest—and is then kept there indefinitely by a mad Englishman so that Tony can read the collected works of Charles Dickens aloud to him.

I had a vision of having to read to my father in Nairobi for the rest of my days.

"No," I said. "I'm going back to London."

MY MOTHER BEING happy enough to have a guest for dinner when Congo was preparing the meal, an Egyptian colleague of Desmond's came over one evening. Dr. Samir Nassif was a tall, burly man, the medical director of Pfizer Egypt. Hearing I was about to return to London, he invited me to break my return journey in Cairo and spend a week with his young family.

It was possible, in those days, to alter an itinerary easily enough, especially when Pfizer paid the penalty for a stopover in Cairo. It was also possible, with a generous host—and Dr. Nassif and his family were extraordinarily generous—to have a sensational time in Cairo without paying for anything. They were members of a sophisticated social circle, and as I didn't have the right clothes for the smart parties they took me to, Madame Nassif even gave me a printed cotton dress that fit like a glove. I had the holiday of a lifetime—and, on the morning of my departure, I spent five pounds for a camel-hide ottoman at the souk. It was a good purchase; half a century later, it sits in my son Adam's living room in Montreal.

ANDY WAS BROKE and had had to borrow money from our landlady to pay the Tube fare to Heathrow to meet me. The five pounds I still had in my pocket was all we had in the world.

It was such a joy to see him again. Such a relief to exchange luxury for a life of poverty with Andy in wintry London.

But Andy was in bad shape, both emotionally and physically, working like a man possessed on a paper he had to prepare for his supervisor of studies, Peter Wiles. His return to Hungary had had a profound impact on him, and he had lost a lot of weight in the two months since we parted in December.

Hungarians, who thought everyone living in the West was rich, expected a returning family member to foot the bill for every meal and every outing. Andy had had little money with him when he arrived in Budapest, he spent every penny while he was there, and he had none left to cover the rent on his return. We now owed our landlady about sixty-five pounds—rent for about eight weeks—which was a small fortune to us. Andy's parents, back in Canada, were unable to provide any more financial help, and I knew better than to ask my parents for money.

Within a week, I was assistant to the marketing manager of Manpower, the head office of an agency that specialized in placing temporary workers in clients' offices across the UK. The pay, which was poor, would cover our living expenses and, if we were careful, it would also allow us to repay our debt over the months to come.

We came up with a tight budget and a weekly shopping list. Pork liver one day, as Andy made a flavourful dish of diced liver sautéed with onions and paprika, then three days of spaghetti Bolognese, and three days of *paprikás krumpli*. The latter, another Andy specialty, consisted mostly of boiled potatoes with fried onion, tomato, paprika, and sliced Hungarian sausage, topped off with a dollop of sour cream. Supplemented with eggs, milk, bread, Marmite, butter, and tea, this was our diet for months. Once a week we went to the local pub and shared one pint of bitter.

It was a meat-heavy diet with little fresh produce, and I got so sick of it that I'm unable, to this day, to eat any of the meals we ate then. We didn't know about cooking with beans and pulses—and spices other than paprika; it was years before I became interested in Indian cooking and discovered a wealth of cheap, nutritious meals, and by that time money was not as scarce as it had been in 1972.

We could find most of the provisions we needed in the supermarket in Muswell Hill, and we bought the most expensive item on our shopping list, ground beef, from whichever butcher had it on sale that week. We had to search further afield for two items needed for *paprikás krumpli*. One was sour cream, which was occasionally available at one delicatessen we knew. The other was Debreceni sausage, then unknown to purveyors of the finest foods in North London. For that, we made our way across London to a Hungarian bookshop that was filled with the rich smell of garlic and smoked pork. There, hanging from the bookcases, were pairs of the Debreceni we wanted.

IT WAS BITTERLY cold in our attic rooms. Not only were the windows not double-glazed, but they were so badly fitted in their frames that the flimsy cotton curtains fluttered indoors on windy days. For heating, we had to feed an electric meter that gobbled shillings at a terrible speed while doing an entirely inadequate job of warming the room. If we sat close enough to feel the heat, we got scorched, and the air was frosty a few inches farther away from the heater. I yelped when Andy touched me with his cold hands, and we both had to wear gloves and socks to bed.

Every morning, delaying the moment when we had to get up and face the cold, we listened to a family of pigeons that had made their home under the roof. Their numbers grew as winter turned to spring, and they were more and more active until, early one morning, the ceiling fell in on top of us, along with the pigeons and feathers and filth.

We moved all our belongings into the other room, and a garbage bag was taped over the gaping hole in the bedroom ceiling.

WE WERE HAPPY. Andy regained his equilibrium and the weight he had lost. He finished his paper on the

New Economic Mechanism that had been developed in postwar Hungary, and Peter Wiles was satisfied. We eventually finished repaying the rent owed. Manpower wanted to keep me on, but I knew I needed to continue my education if I were to find work I enjoyed.

I was accepted into the MPhil program at Queen Mary College, which, like the London School of Economics, is one of the colleges of the University of London. A few weeks later, Andy and I got news that both our applications to the Quebec research funding agency had been successful. It had been tough, but we now knew we were going to make it.

ANDY RETURNED TO Hungary that summer, and I joined him on the Croatian coast, where we spent a week before travelling to Budapest by train. I knew little Hungarian during that first visit to Hungary, but I longed to learn. I started with a language text, and with the patient help of Zsuzsa, the wife of one of Andy's many cousins. Zsuzsa also taught me how to cook *bableves, gulyásleves*, and other Hungarian soups I loved.

On our return to London in August, the hole in the bedroom ceiling had still not been repaired, and we moved into a house down the hill on Priory Road in Crouch End. A rock musician and his girlfriend lived downstairs. Andy and I shared the upstairs flat with another student from Montreal and his English girlfriend—and with Ian, who flew in from Nairobi with a suitcase full of Kenyan coffee. He had been forced on short notice to get out of Kenya, as he lacked the papers required to work there.

Had Nan and Desmond succeeded in getting me to stay in Nairobi in February, it would clearly not have been for long. If I had done what my parents wanted, abandoning Andy, it's unclear how he'd have survived the winter in London. I'd have lost my place at Queen Mary College, too, as there was no way my grant would have been transferable to Nairobi.

And for what? With no working papers and no way of getting any, I too would have been forced out of Kenya.

My parents had been desperate to keep the family together, and now it was breaking up in spite of all their efforts.

I was the villain of the piece, not for the first time and not for the last. We all play roles in our families, and I was now the black sheep of the family.

Sure enough, Desmond had been complaining about me on 1st Ngong Avenue. I learned this from Brian, who'd been concerned by what he'd heard Desmond say about me in Nairobi, and who soon followed Ian to London. I tried, with Andy's help—he had no family history of silence and was not intimidated by Desmond—to respond to these complaints in a carefully thought-out letter.

Desmond, that master of concision, replied with a telegram of just three words: *Over and out.*

Which is how I got disowned for the second time.

I LOVED BEING a student again. I delved into Beckett's work in the fall of 1972, and over the next two years read more widely and more deeply than I ever did before or since. This led me to Joyce, who had been a friend of Beckett's. One of Beckett's early essays is entitled "Dante Bruno Vico Joyce," so then I read Dante and Bruno and Vico, taking long detours through aesthetics and art history, theories of comedy, literary theory, post-structuralism, Wittgenstein, and Buster Keaton.

Beckett's thesis on Proust interested me especially, and I read his account of the workings of involuntary memory many times, in attempts to understand its transformative effect. I took a train from London to the University of Reading, which had the (then) unpublished manuscript of Beckett's first novel, "Dream of Fair to Middling Women." Andy and I spent countless hours in the Reading Room of the British Library in Bloomsbury.

I met periodically with my academic supervisor at Queen Mary College, Charles Peake, and spent one or two afternoons a week at the Tate Gallery or the National Gallery, attending lectures on the collections and on current exhibitions. I read every word of the weekly *Times Literary Supplement* and followed the literary columnists and book, movie, and art reviews in the *Guardian.* I spent many afternoons at Oxfam book-shops with Andy and Ian, buying second-hand books to fill in gaps in my reading. Ian, who had been studying the work of architectural historian Nikolaus Pevsner, led us on enjoyable and informative walks across London.

THEN NAN CALLED from Nairobi to say that Desmond had had another breakdown on a trip to Johannesburg, and that this one was more serious than the one that had precipitated the departure from Brussels. He needed psychiatric treatment in London, she said. Could he spend a few days with us on Priory Road?

He could.

Desmond flew to London and then, after a spell in hospital, he moved in with us for several months. We had many discussions during his stay, many good meals—he cooked a standing rib roast of beef for Christmas dinner in our tiny oven—and not a few arguments, disagreeing about politics, religion, the state of Britain, Vietnam, feminism, everything. He was drinking heavily—I had to ask him to pay for the bottles of Johnny Walker we bought for him almost every day—and he was volatile. Angered one evening by a feminist argument I made, he retorted, "You're not a woman!" It was meant to be a zinger, but it failed to zing. The old warrior was losing his power.

BRIAN, WHO WAS at Queen Elizabeth College, had a flat in central London. Sheelagh and Mandy came to stay with us, en route to Headington School in Oxford. The last in the procession of family visitors were Nan and dear old Granny Jo, who arrived in the summer.

The kitchen was overcrowded, and our limited furnishings were not up to the challenge. The wooden fold-out chair in the living room was pressed into service, and Sheelagh was unlucky enough to be the one sleeping on that.

There weren't enough dishes, and there wasn't enough bedding, but we were in the midst of a heat wave, so blankets weren't needed. That was the good news. The bad news was that the heat had brought out an infestation of tiny insects, which did not improve our reputation with Nan. It was a full house.

I HAD BEEN living in a remarkably impersonal state of intellectual and literary excitement. Beckett was a towering literary figure whose work I admired immeasurably, but I didn't love him or his work. It didn't hurt that he was an Irishman, certainly, but I felt no closeness to him, and no warmth. He was such an austere character that the work leading to my doctorate from the University of London—I moved from the MPhil to the PhD program in 1973—was intellectually stimulating without really mattering all that much to me.

That's what I thought.

A New Life

Andy and I were both looking forward to returning to Montreal and finding work. My parents had given up their attempts to get me to move back home, wherever home happened to be. They left Nairobi in 1974 and resettled in Brussels, where Pfizer had found a less pressured job for Desmond.

Andy wanted us to marry, an idea I resisted. The only reason I could see for marriage was if we were to have a baby. Happy as I was with our common-law relationship—Andy was my love, my ally, my soulmate, and the main reason I had had the strength to resist my parents—my objections to marriage were weakening. There had been two occasions when I thought I might be pregnant. The first time, I was hugely relieved to learn it was a false alarm. The second time was another false alarm, but this time, I was disappointed to learn I was not pregnant after all.

For three years, ever since I left Paris, I had been moving in the direction of a different kind of existence from any I had dreamed of. Instead of the bohemian life, I was heading for an academic career and a family of my own, and the oddest thing is that that is what I now wanted.

It was more than that, for a family of my own, children of my own, now felt like a necessity.

I didn't give Madame de Staël a moment's thought, so I didn't remind myself that the grande dame herself had had four children. In any case, motherhood had been an entirely different proposition for Staël, with her wealth and her many servants—not to mention her lovers—than it would ever be for me. For us, Andy and me. For my one stipulation, when I agreed to marriage, was that he and I should continue to share domestic responsibilities fifty-fifty. I wanted nothing to change.

That was wishful thinking, for everything changed, and I was soon living a life not entirely unlike my mother's.

I should have known.

And of course, I did know, but I went ahead anyway.

My relationship with Andy felt solid, so that was certainly a reason for marrying him. My newfound desire for children played a part of it, too. A hope that I'd manage to live out my dreams in the throes of pregnancy and childbirth and child-raising. That I would continue to be the person I had been. And become the person I wanted to be.

Instead, I became a woman I scarcely recognized in the mirror. It felt necessary to be that woman, when I was in my twenties and thirties. I convinced myself that was the woman my children needed me to be—and the woman I myself now needed to be. I wasn't wrong about that, for I did grow and mature in this new role.

It was a role, certainly, but it felt natural. I had grown up looking after other members of my family. I was good at doing that, and it felt right to have a family of my own to look after.

For the truth is that I wanted to be the woman I saw in the mirror. But I wanted to be more than that, as well.

My dreams hadn't died, even if it sometimes felt as though they had. I was wistful about that, occasionally desperate. I hadn't learned to pace myself. I didn't even know yet that I would eventually be able to write. I had no way of knowing there would be times when I would write, and times my life would make it impossible to write.

At that moment, aged twenty-four, I had a life to live, and I wanted to get on with it.

SO, ANDY AND I were married in London in July 1974. My whole family was staying with us on Priory Road for the occasion, and Andy and I spent a couple of weeks in the house my parents had rented in central Brussels. We flew back to Montreal in August, and Andy's parents had a party for us in Sainte-Anne-de-Bellevue. Instead of settling in Montreal, though, we then moved to Ottawa, where Andy had a one-year appointment at Carleton University, and I did my first paid work as an editor on a collection of academic essays by geographers.

We had been anxious to return to Montreal, and we were happy when Andy took up a position in the Political Science Department at Concordia University the following year, and I started teaching in the English Department of John Abbott College.

I visited my family in Brussels at Christmas, 1975, and Andy returned to Budapest. He and I then spent a few days in London, where I defended my thesis in a small classroom at University College. This was a modest occasion, but nonetheless an occasion, and I had dressed for it in navy blue, top to toe, a suede skirt, turtleneck top, and matching tights and shoes. Not at all my usual colour—I have rarely worn navy blue, before or since—but it seemed appropriate.

So, it was with a smile of recognition that I saw the British classicist Mary Beard's account of her first interview for an academic job, a couple years after my thesis defence. She had bought herself a pair of blue tights specially for the occasion. "It wasn't my usual fashion choice," she writes in *Women & Power*, "but the logic was satisfying: 'If your interviewers are going to be thinking that I'm a right bluestocking, let me just show you that I *know* that's what you're thinking *and* that I got there first.'"[16]

Looking up the word "bluestocking" today, I see the usual definitions—and the usual disparagement of intellectual women. And I see that William Hazlitt's opinion was that "the bluestocking is the most odious character in society." Hazlitt having been one of the most misogynist characters of his day, I wonder who at Penguin Random House held him in sufficiently high regard to name their online imprint after him.

MY WORK ON Beckett was now done, and I put it aside. Inspired by Mr. Baker's recommendations of Montreal writers and by my old history teacher Dr. Smith's enthusiasm for Canada, I became a Canadian citizen and resolved to immerse myself in Canadian writing. This was where I would be making my home, and I couldn't imagine being unfamiliar with the writing of the society I was part of.

I plunged into this new subject with great energy, reading widely, subscribing to publications that reviewed Canadian books, and signing up for a newsletter promoting new releases. It was a perfect time to be doing this, with Canadian literature garnering significant attention for the first time.

As I quickly discovered, though, CanLit had its centre of gravity in Toronto, where most of the publishing houses and media were based. CanLit was also written in English, with very occasional nods in the direction of Canadian writers working in French. Living in Montreal, I was interested in work written and published in French, too.

The first Canadian writer who got my full attention was Marie-Claire Blais, whose surreal debut novel, *La Belle bête*, was written when Blais was in her teens. I had read *The Apprenticeship of Duddy Kravitz*, one of the books Mr. Baker had drawn my attention to in high school, and I now read more of Mordecai Richler's work as well as a wide range of other fiction by such writers as Hugh MacLennan, Gabrielle Roy, Margaret Laurence, Leonard Cohen, Margaret Atwood, Harold Sonny Ladoo, Hubert Aquin, Michael Ondaatje, Matt Cohen, Carol Shields, Alice Munro, Anne Hébert, Marian Engel, and countless others. This was a rich vein to mine, and I admire much of this work to this day. I soon discovered, though, that the writers who interested me most were the Quebec writers.

THE LIVELIEST, THE best, and the wittiest of Canadian writers, Mavis Gallant had intrigued me from the first time I happened across her story "Bernadette," about a French-Canadian servant in an upper-middle-class Montreal household.

Gallant lived in Paris, not very far from Beckett, though he had long been writing in French; Mavis wrote in English and lived in French. I was impressed by the ability of both these writers to sail over linguistic barriers, and by the intelligence and liveliness of Gallant's work. There was something appealing, too, about the fact that she was so little known in Canada—that only changed after 1982—so that she felt like a writer I had discovered for myself.

I had been teaching a course on utopian and anti-utopian literature inspired by my Marxist undergraduate professor, Darko Suvin, who had introduced me to alternative imaginary worlds at McGill. I regularly taught a course on the short story, too. I now included "Bernadette" alongside work by Mordecai Richler, Leonard Cohen, Norman Levine, and Gail Scott, in a course I designed on the writers of English Montreal.

So, I was riveted by the six stories about Linnet Muir that Mavis published in *The New Yorker* in the mid- and late 1970s. This was a treasure trove for a reader intent on scanning fiction for autobiographical material.

Reading Mavis was not without its perils, however. In one of these Montreal stories, "In Youth Is Pleasure," the young Linnet Muir is living on the Lakeshore over the summer months while working downtown. Thinking about her future, she decides that one thing she absolutely does not want to be is the "sensitive housewife in the suburbs."

That stung. I read "In Youth Is Pleasure" in the house that Andy and I bought on the Lakeshore just after our second son, Michael, was born in 1978. Improbably enough, this house at 52 Golf Avenue is just a few doors up the hill from the house at 40 Golf Avenue I had lived in with my parents in the 1960s. Was it any wonder that I could see myself turning into my mother?

Mavis never wanted to be the sensitive housewife in the suburbs, and I had never wanted that, either. And I wasn't a housewife, I told myself defensively; I did have a doctorate, after all, not to mention a full-time tenured academic position and a small but growing list of publications.

Gallant's dismissive comment was still too close for comfort, especially when I was on maternity leave, nursing newborn Michael, and watching *The Friendly Giant* with eighteen-month-old Adam beside me.

THE CANADA COUNCIL was offering a short-lived "Explorations" program for emerging writers to which I applied in 1979. I was proposing to write about Mavis Gallant's work, not to write fiction of my own, but this was a step forward, nonetheless. The application was successful, and this was the first in a series of grants I got in the 1980s and early 1990s that moved me deeper into the literary world.

I wrote an article about Gallant's Montreal stories for a new magazine, *Montreal Review*, which two of my English department colleagues were starting up. I then wrote to Mavis herself, who had a reputation for being testy. I approached her with trepidation, telling her about my article and asking her a few questions about the stories.

To my horror, she threatened to sue me if I so much as suggested there was anything autobiographical about the stories. Her accusation stunned me, but she was not far off the mark, for I had been looking for every scrap of information about her life I could glean from her stories.

And I wasn't far off the mark, either, for these six stories are very close to being autobiographical. It wasn't long after firing off that angry letter to me that Mavis herself described the Linnet Muir stories as being "as autobiographical as it is possible for fiction to be."

I sent her the finished article with a polite note a few weeks later, shortly before the first issue of *Montreal Review* went to print. She wrote back a friendly letter thanking me and praising the piece. "What a relief!" she said.

So, we got over that.

USING FUNDS FROM my grant, I went to Paris to meet Mavis in May 1980. She suggested tea, and I made my way to her apartment on rue Jean-Ferrandi at the appointed hour. I had wondered what I should bring as an offering and decided on a bottle of Tio Pepe. We opened it at once.

Mavis's work on Alfred Dreyfus had been occupying her for several years, and we talked about that. She closed the door to her living room to show me the newspaper cover with Zola's *J'accuse*, explaining that she kept it behind the door to protect it from the damaging effect of light.

She was curious about me, and I told her about my schooling and about my thesis on Beckett. She approved. She wanted to know what I'd done since getting to Paris, and I told her about the Fassbinder film I'd been to see earlier that afternoon. I had chosen the film because I knew from an interview with Mavis that she admired Fassbinder, and I thought she might have seen his new film. I had been moved, I told her, by the scene in which the main female character said, "*Mein Mann ist tod*"— my husband is dead. She nodded, but she hadn't seen the film.

We talked about Brian Moore, whom she had known in Montreal and didn't like; she had been close to his first wife, the journalist Jackie Sirois, and didn't like the way he had treated her. We talked about Quebec politics, as Montrealers away from home do. The conversation sailed, in other words, and it was three hours later, the bottle of sherry not quite empty, when I got up to go. I would have given anything to continue, to invite her to dinner, but I didn't want to outstay my welcome.

Mavis and I corresponded regularly after that. I took her to lunch or to dinner when she was in Montreal, once at her old haunt, the Ritz, and later at Les Halles. I had lunch with her on later trips to Paris. I saw her in Toronto when she was writer-in-residence at the University of Toronto.

Sheelagh read Mavis's stories, too, and commented on how funny they are. It was a good reminder, as I'd been so seriously focused on my writing about her fiction that I had forgotten simply to enjoy its wit and mischief.

When my third son, Julian, was born in 1982, Mavis wrote a lovely, effusive note to him, in which she invited him to a party that would take place seventeen years later, on New Year's Eve, 1999. (He loved this idea, when he was growing up, and was disappointed, in 1999, when it became clear that Mavis had forgotten her promise.)

SOME PART OF me loved this new life, and some part of me wanted the life I had dreamed of. When I was a girl of four and five, and Desmond was leading the life of an editor in Bloomsbury, I had adored the idea of being in the thick of it. When I was twelve and thirteen, I loved translating Latin poetry. At seventeen, I was intrigued by Adolphe and Ellénore and Madame de Staël. Being intrigued isn't a criterion much used by literary critics, but I have long found it the surest way of knowing I have to read more by a writer and find out more about them.

I was not writing, in this new life, and I had nothing remotely like a literary salon. I led a Norman Rockwell–style suburban life with my husband, our three sons, a handsome yellow Lab called Hector, and a good job.

I was head over heels in love with my children. I taught them to read and I took them to the library to choose books for them—and, soon enough, Adam insisted on choosing books for himself. I took them to music classes at Stewart Hall, and Michael went to a neighbour's house for art classes and made the clay figures that sit on my kitchen shelf to this day. I sang to them the songs I had learned from Granny Jo.

I hung out with them at the outdoor pool all summer long, summer after summer, where I swam lengths with my friend Liz during adult swim, and accompanied my sons to swim meets in the evenings and on weekends. Michael was unusually good at the butterfly stroke, which I had always found exhausting, and Adam at the Australian crawl. They had all absorbed the Hungarian love of soccer, and Julian excelled as centre forward, scoring goal after goal all through high school. Andy and I spent balmy summer evenings in suburban parks watching him play and chatting with the other parents.

It was a busy and sociable time, crowded with friends and family. The architect and political dissident László Rajk, who was spending a few months in New York City, came up to see us on Golf Avenue. Other Hungarian friends, and friends of friends, stopped by for a few days. Brian, now a presenter with the BBC's Natural History unit in Bristol, did a fall fly-past. Sheelagh, who had married a research scientist from Northern Ireland named Willie Taylor, flew over from London with their beautiful baby girl. At the start of a cross-Canada trip, Mandy and her boyfriend came to stay.

We saw Ian a few times, too, especially during the months he was living in New York with his girlfriend, Susie, who happened to be related to Willie. When Ian and Susie went their separate ways, she came up to see us on her own, and we had a big party in the garden to welcome her.

We did little travelling in those years, though we did spend a fun New Year's Eve with Susie in New York. Andy had taken on some consulting work that kept him in Toronto for a spell, and by the mid-1980s he had started returning to Budapest. On two ill-fated occasions I went to see my family, and I made it to a couple of academic conferences as well as spending time with Margaret and her husband and newborn son in Vancouver.

MY MARRIAGE WAS starting to buckle, however, under the pressures of children, work, and domestic responsibilities. Far from sharing those responsibilities fifty-fifty, I was doing the lion's share. I was unhappy, and I feared for the future.

It was in this state that I decided to take my children on a visit to my parents, who had moved to Canterbury by this time. I had to reconsider my future, and I needed to be looked after.

Did I really think my parents would look after me? I should have known better.

Had I forgotten that my role in the family was to look after others? Thinking about the challenges of the journey, with young children, I couldn't see how I could negotiate Heathrow, and the airport bus and the walk up to Victoria Station, the train journey to Canterbury, and finally the walk from the train to the house on Stour Street. I asked if my mother—who had a car she used for antiquing—could meet me at Heathrow.

No, she couldn't. What she could do was drive two minutes to meet the train at Canterbury West.

That dashed some of my hopes. I did my best to understand why that might be—and yes, I did know it was a long drive to Heathrow on busy roads, but I was making an effort and I thought she could, too.

I should have cancelled my trip then and there, but that didn't occur to me, and it would certainly have entailed a financial penalty. I wanted to see Granny Jo, now elderly, I wanted to see my brothers and sisters, and I wanted to introduce them all to my children.

Dear Ian met me at Heathrow and helped us on the journey to Canterbury. When we arrived, I was appalled by the creepy listed property my parents had bought in the centre of Canterbury—and I was shocked by my father's lack of interest in his only grandchildren.

My parents had met Adam once, in Brussels, when he was an infant. Nan now took him in hand, to his evident dismay; he was not used to her brisk discipline. Skeptical about my claim that he was able to read—he was three years old—she sat with him and tested his skills until she eventually admitted that, yes, he could read.

Nan and Desmond had been uneven parents, and they didn't seem at all sure about being grandparents.

Desmond especially wanted my boys out of his way. These were very small children, entirely out of their element. The dark portrait of Napoleon that had hung in the living room at 40 Golf Avenue was now upstairs, where the old warrior's eyes seemed to glitter when we made our way to the bathroom.

"They can play in the garden," Desmond announced when we arrived. I stepped outside gingerly. There was a small patch of ground on two levels with a few blades of grass, but it was studded with shards of glass and pottery from an archeological dig that had unearthed Roman remains.

"They can play in the drawing room," Desmond suggested next. There were two sofas in the drawing room, but the antique glass-fronted cabinet was filled with cut glass goblets, bone china figurines, and dozens of tchotchkes with price stickers attached. I could read to my sons and play with them there, but I couldn't leave them on their own.

Desmond wanted me to keep him company in the kitchen and was incensed when I said I couldn't leave the boys to their own devices in the drawing room. "You're spoiling them," he said.

I should have known that my idea of childcare and his were poles apart. I had known that. When I was expecting Adam, I had sworn not to raise my children the way my parents had raised me.

"You're bringing them up to be juvenile delinquents," he said.

It had been such a mistake to come home.

I moved mountains and spent money I didn't have to return to Montreal before the scheduled date. Ian, who lived in London, came down by train to help me on the journey back through London to Heathrow.

I don't know how I would have made it on my own. My boys were rowdy on that trip and on the flight back to Montreal, too; they must have sensed something was wrong, as children do. I was in despair.

So, my parents and I were estranged, yet again. Did they write at all over the next couple of years? Did they call? I don't think so. I myself wrote occasionally and stopped by to see them once, for a couple of days, en route to a Canadian studies conference in Southampton.

ANDY AND I found ourselves a therapist, who turned out to be a kind Brazilian woman named Letty. We both knew how close we had come to separating, and we both learned a great deal from her about the cultural differences that had been complicating the usual mix of domestic issues.

Andy had been inviting people to our house unexpectedly—a single colleague he brought home for dinner, a dozen or more people he invited to a party at our house—without saying a word to me. Coming from a large, gregarious family, he saw no need to let me know, let alone consult me, and he didn't get it when I tried to explain why this drove me round the bend.

Letty understood why I was so irked, but suggested it would be a good idea for me to speak out, at the time, about what was bothering me instead of suffering in silence. I could see the wisdom in this, and I knew exactly how I'd picked up the habit of suffering in silence. She convinced me that Andy's behaviour was natural enough in his culture and suggested he take my own family background into consideration.

Making some adjustments to our behaviour and our expectations of each other, Andy and I soldiered on, but we had lost the boundless hope and confidence of our early years together.

SO, WHEN I think of those days with my beautiful boys, I remember them as an idyll—but I wasn't always happy. Andy and I looked, to most of the people who knew us, as an ideal and enviable couple. And I myself had it all, yes, sort of. All except the literary career I wanted.

There was little I could do about that. My time was fully occupied with family life and teaching. My dreams were on hold—had been on hold for years already, during the years of study in London, the years of teaching, the years of having babies. As those babies grew, I started channelling those literary desires into reviewing for the book trade monthly *Quill and Quire*, the left-wing magazine *The Canadian Forum*, and the academic journal *Essays on Canadian Writing*. That was as much as I could manage.

We had a hefty mortgage, and interest rates were historically high, even though we had benefitted from a relatively low purchase price as a result of the exodus of Anglos from nationalist Quebec. I drove west from Golf Avenue to work at John Abbott College—which shared the Macdonald College campus in Sainte-Anne-de-Bellevue—while Andy headed east to Concordia, so we had two cars and all the other expenses of a big household.

BESIDES, I HAD tried living the life of a writer when I was in Paris and London, and that had gotten me nowhere.

It did not seem possible to think of giving up my teaching job, and I knew of no job that would be a better fit while my children were young. John Abbott is one of Quebec's post-secondary colleges, or Cegeps, which offer a professional program as well as a more academic program for students planning to go to university. Vacations were long, I enjoyed the mix of students, my colleagues were friendly, and the hours flexible enough that I could do preparatory work and marking at home with my boys.

It had always been important to me to have an income of my own, and that became increasingly important when Andy and I started having difficulties in our marriage. Concern that the marriage might not last waxed and waned over many years.

What to do? I needed my job, and I wanted to write. It's a quandary familiar to many writers, especially literary women, and it can be agonizing for those with children. It was no contest at all in my case, though, for I couldn't pretend to be a writer.

I seldom had enough time and space and energy to sit down with a notebook and pen. I was trying to write short stories, but this was not a form I felt at home in. What I really wanted was to write a novel, but how on earth could I do that? I didn't know how I would ever write again.

Literary Women

It's a mercy that I had not, at that point, seen the short BBC documentary about Muriel Spark that shows the author sitting at a desk, in profile, with a thick stack of manuscript pages in front of her. She looks to be in her early fifties, and she's wearing a crisp, candy-striped shirt, very brisk and professional.

"I begin at the beginning," she says. "I write my name on the first page." She looks at the manuscript, then corrects herself. "I write the title, then I write my name. Then I turn over and write 'Chapter One,' and then I write on."

She picks up the stack of pages and flips through them so we can see how they're marked with a few doodles and scribbles. "I leave a space so I can make alterations as I go along," she explains. She sets the pile of papers down again on the desk and looks up at the off-camera interviewer. "But I don't revise it afterwards."

"Then it goes to the typist," she says, "and she types it. And I revise that. And that's the book. That's finished."

It's a delicious few minutes, and I'd have been crushed if I'd seen it when I was a young mother frustrated by my inability to write.

The *Guardian*'s description of Spark's method is equally discouraging to a novice writer, even if slightly different: Spark writes "in copperplate handwriting, straight out in a single draft, into special spiral-bound notebooks imported from the Edinburgh stationers, James Thin. On one side of the paper only."[17] It's a very good thing that I'd managed to publish half a dozen books by the time I read that in Spark's obituary in 2006.[18]

Writing a book is not nearly as simple as Muriel Spark makes it sound, however. Not for most of us, anyway. Before she got into stride, Sparks had herself faced many challenges in becoming a writer. She divorced her husband, left her son to be raised by her parents, suffered an emotional breakdown, and converted to Catholicism before publishing her first novel at the age of thirty-nine.

I LOVED MEMOIRS, autobiographies, and collections of letters as well as fiction I thought autobiographical. While my little boys were choosing the books they'd bring home from the library, I was seeking out what I myself wanted to read. I admired Sylvia Plath's *The Bell Jar*, Françoise Sagan's *Bonjour Tristesse*, Jean Rhys's *Wide Sargasso Sea*, and everything Margaret Drabble wrote.

I read and reread Drabble's early novels—*A Summer Bird-Cage, The Garrick Year, The Millstone*—as though every word were not only true, but addressed to me personally. A talented and accomplished woman with a degree from Cambridge, Drabble knew all about the challenges of combining motherhood and a career. With three children to bring up, she had somehow managed to become a celebrated novelist. There was a husband, who was an actor, and I was not surprised when I learned they eventually divorced.

The writers who mattered to me were all older than I was—Margaret Drabble and Margaret Atwood are about ten years my senior—and the ones who mattered most—Muriel Spark, Doris Lessing, and Mavis Gallant—were from my mother's generation. They all had something in common with me, as well, in their familiarity with corners of the world once controlled by the British, and in their daring to go their own ways.

Mavis had become a friend, and I never met Muriel Spark, but I did meet Doris Lessing several times on visits to Edinburgh at festival time. During one conversation with her in the yurt, which is where the authors and hosts congregate before and after their events, she and I had a long conversation about *Medical World*, about my parents, the Communist Party of Great Britain in the 1950s, and the collective of communist doctors that included one of Nan's admirers, Hugh Faulkner—who, it turned out, had been Doris's own doctor in those years.

I admire younger writers, too—Zadie Smith and Rachel Cusk among them—and the work of many who have entirely different kinds of experience from my own—E.M. Forster, Graham Greene, Bharati Mukherjee, Toni Morrison, Magda Szabó, to name a few—and some who have spent their whole lives in just one kind of place.

The writers who interest me most, always, are women who write about themselves in ways that a male writer never could: not even Nabokov, masterful though his memoir—*Speak, Memory: An Autobiography*

Revisited—is. Certainly not Beckett, who never wrote a memoir, and whose work forbids autobiographical speculation.[19]

A WOMAN'S LIFE is often complicated in ways that a man's life is not. And, however complicated the circumstances—which might include such challenges as poverty, inadequate education, a bad marriage, the responsibilities of motherhood, not to mention social upheaval, cataclysm, and war—a woman's life is complicated in ways that one woman may have in common with other women and is less likely to have in common with a man.

As soon as I started reading one of these women, I wanted to know how she became the writer she had become.

Where was she born? Into what kind of world? What did she think of that world? Was she happy there? Or was she itching to leave?

The answers to many of these questions were not yet readily available, though the avalanche of feminist scholarship has since filled in some of the gaps. With few biographies in print, few critical studies, no useful bibliography—and no Internet—these women's own writings were my main resource. I read on, in the hope of finding answers. To this day, I read and reread the books that matter to me until they fall apart, and I never part with them, though the pages turn yellow and are held together by elastic bands.

What kind of parents did she have? What kind of education? Was the family supportive? Disapproving? Dysfunctional?

What prospects did she have when she was growing up? What were her dreams?

What contact did she have with boys? With men? With women? What, if anything, did she have to say about sex? About her own sexuality? (Often very little.)

Did she marry, or not? And, if she did marry—as Spark, Lessing, and Gallant all did—how long did she stay married? (Not long.)

Did she have lovers? Did she have a child? More than one child? This spoke to me directly. It was when Muriel Spark and Doris Lessing published their memoirs that I realized there was another question—did she raise the child herself? Spark and Lessing both left their sons in others' care as they struggled to make a literary career for themselves. I could not imagine doing that.

And how did she become a writer? Was she encouraged? (Rarely.)

Or was she silenced?

WE ALL KNOW stories about girls and women who kept quiet, even if it killed them. Mary Beard writes about Hera and Penelope, who were told to shut up, about a Roman woman described as "barking," and about Philomela, whose tongue was cut out so she could never tell anyone she had been raped."[20]

There are modern examples, too, from Anita Hill to Alexandria Ocasio-Cortez. Few are bold enough to stand up to the fear of speaking out—and to pay the price of being heard.

In the Norwegian fairy tale "The Twelve Wild Ducks," the princess is set almost insurmountable perils in her attempt to save her twelve brothers. Her life depends not only on her goodness and her determination, but also on her silence.

AND IF, AGAINST all odds, a woman did eventually manage to succeed in saying what she had to say, I wanted to find out how she got her work published.

Did she spend years looking for a way in? Did she self-publish? Or did she pull a story out of a picnic hamper, as Mavis did, type it up, and get an encouraging response from *The New Yorker* on that first submission— before the editors accepted the second story she sent in?

When did she get published? Was she young? Was it decades before she finally made it?

And how was her work received? Was it taken seriously? Was she belittled and demeaned?

Was she ever not?

Did she doubt herself? Did she ever wonder if she really had any talent as a writer? I was astonished to hear Mavis voice that very question when she took the stage during the vast tribute to her work held in 2006 at New York's Symphony Space.

I HAD A great interest in financial considerations, as well.

Was she able to support herself by writing? (Sometimes.)

Was there family money she could depend on? (Hardly ever.)

Did she have a supportive husband bringing home the bacon? (Occasionally. And occasionally the marriage did last.)

Did she live in penury? (Yes, in many cases.)

Or did she have some other paid work and somehow still find the time, energy, and courage to write her books? (Yes, often.)

SOME OF THESE questions may seem to belong to the past, to the bad old days before there was much awareness of the difficulties women so often face in their quest for an income from their writing. Today, surely, times have changed, and these are no longer questions as pressing as they were to the young Muriel Spark, the young Doris Lessing, and the young Mavis Gallant.

Not so.

It is harder now than it was when they were starting out. Writers' incomes have plummeted. Opportunities for publishing in magazines and newspapers—many writers' mainstay in the past—are now vanishingly rare. Publishers' advances are a fraction of what they used to be, when there's any advance at all, and fiction is now a tough sell.

I HAD NO family money. I was earning more or less the same as my husband, barely enough to cover our expenses. I had three children I could never think of abandoning. I wasn't ready to divorce. I wanted to write, and I had no reason to believe I would ever be able to do so.

Several of my John Abbott colleagues were published writers—Peter van Toorn, David Solway, Claudia Morrison, Kenneth Radu, Endre Farkas, Ruth Taylor— and at least one of them had enrolled in the Creative Writing program at Concordia, not in order to better his writing but to increase his earnings with an MFA. I considered doing the same, in order to better my writing, but soon dismissed the idea. I didn't have money for tuition, and I couldn't add to my to-do list. Besides, I hadn't written much of anything in years. I was chagrined to admit it, but I had nothing recent I could be proud to include in a portfolio.

So that was no solution. I had to keep teaching, and somehow find a way of getting back to writing. Of writing better. Of becoming a writer.

Changing

I planned a visit to Canterbury in the hope of reconciling with my parents. I would take Adam, now eight, leaving Michael and Julian with Andy and his parents. Adam and I would spend a short time in Canterbury, where Mandy was still at home with my parents, and I'd be able to visit Granny Jo, who was in a nursing home. We'd head up to London, too, to see Sheelagh and Ian, then visit Brian in Bristol.

It was another ill-fated trip. Adam and I were scheduled to leave Montreal on December 12, 1984, and my mother called on December 11 to let me know that she had come home from shopping to find Desmond dead in his armchair. He had had a fatal heart attack.

How could he die on the very eve of my return? It was too cruel.

I arrived on my birthday. My brothers and sisters were already in Canterbury for the funeral, and I got to see my dear Granny Jo for the last time. Daddy's brother, Raymond, and his wife, Peggy, came over from

Northern Ireland. They were jolly and relaxed, and Raymond always had a special word for me. That was the last time I saw him, too.

Adam and I did get to London, as well—where he kept a notebook on a long ride across the city on the top of a double-decker bus—and out to Bristol, where I developed a fear of heights at the prospect of crossing the Clifton Suspension Bridge.

I was devastated by grief. By disbelief, too, and regret, and a sorrow I could not imagine ever emerging from. In some ways I never have.

BUT THAT'S NOT the whole story.

My father's death was the beginning of a great change in my life. It was ten years since Andy and I had returned to Canada, and our years on Golf Avenue had provided me with more stability than I had ever known—geographically, emotionally, personally, professionally—but the seeds of change had now been sown.

A change in how I thought about my father, about my mother, about my marriage, about myself; a series of changes in my professional life; a move from one house to another, then from one country to another and back again; the revival of the dreams I'd had when I was seventeen, and the fulfilment of those dreams.

It's a process of change that has lasted ever since.

QUEBEC WAS NOW offering grants that provided a small number of college researchers with a fully paid leave of absence from teaching for up to three years. Inspired by the course I had been teaching on fiction written in English by writers in Montreal and elsewhere in Quebec, I developed an ambitious new project and prepared a grant application. I was incredulous, at first, when I got the news that my application was successful, and then I was ecstatic. My first move was to set up a home office for myself, complete with a spiffy Ikea desk, a good chair, a filing cabinet, and stationery. Banal as this now seems, I was thrilled to have a budget for such expenditures and thrilled by the door this grant opened up for me.

And that was before I had any way of knowing which door that really was. The period I was interested in started with the publication of Hugh MacLennan's *Two Solitudes,* in 1945, and with Mavis Gallant, who worked as a journalist in Montreal in the 1940s. It included Mordecai Richler and Leonard Cohen—to mention only those—before focusing on writers living and working here in the 1970s and 1980s.

Very little had been written about the younger writers, so much of my research consisted in reading novels, stories, and such reviews as I could find. It also included interviewing these writers as well as journalists, critics, and other commentators. I was my own boss, in a field with no precedent, paid a full-time salary to make my own way in an obscure and little understood literary milieu that had never previously attracted scholarly attention.

So I knew that, in freeing me from teaching for three years, the grant would open doors to the writers and their work. That itself was an exciting prospect, but there were bigger questions. What writers? What work? And how did they and their work relate to one another, to their readers, and to the world around them?

At the start, in 1985, I was a college teacher and occasional book reviewer; by the time the project wrapped up, three years later, I had become an active member of the literary milieu. The door that grant opened for me was the door to a world I wanted to be part of.

MAVIS'S STAR HAD risen after her collection of Canadian stories, *Home Truths,* was published in 1982, and I went to Toronto in November of that year for the premiere of her play *What Is To Be Done?* at the Tarragon Theatre. She was invited to numerous events in Canada, especially in Toronto and Montreal, and I invited her to John Abbott for a reading to my students and colleagues. I showed her what I had written about her fiction, and she was noncommittal about that, as she always was about commentary on her work.

I told her about my research project, and she loved the idea of someone writing about Montreal in the 1940s. "It was unique," she said, when I interviewed her about that time. "It was a wonderful, thrilling time to be young. All the old conservative dead weight was still there, and of course French Canada was still locked, but there were elements breaking out, and that was what was so exciting."[21] She referred me to some old friends and colleagues I might interview. I already knew William Weintraub, who himself later wrote *City Unique* (1996) on the Montreal of the 1940s and 1950s and *Getting Started: Memoirs of the 1950s* (2001), which chronicles his friendships with Mordecai Richler, Brian Moore, and Mavis.

IN 1985, I also went back to Hungary with Andy, renewing old acquaintance with László. He had become active in the opposition to the communist regime, and I got to know other artists and intellectuals in his circle.

Several of them came to New York in the 1980s on fellowships funded by the George Soros foundation, and when they did, they paid us a visit in Montreal. We hosted dinners for most of them at one time or another either on Golf Avenue or at a ski house we rented in the Eastern Townships.

I used to throw dinner parties readily, in those days. Another guest was Mavis herself, on a visit to Montreal, when I invited her out to Golf Avenue for dinner with a few friends. She met my sons, taking a particular interest in Julian, and went out of her way to talk to Andy.

It must have been Andy who tucked the boys into bed that evening, as I was preoccupied with the meal. I have no recollection of what I cooked for the occasion, but Andy's mother had made a glorious hazelnut torte we served for dessert. The friend who drove Mavis to and from our house was foolhardy enough to ask her several questions that earned him a sharp rebuke when Mavis turned to ask, "Are you interviewing me?"

I had had my own experience of Mavis's sharp tongue, of course, before I'd even met her. After that baptism by fire, though, and especially after the bottle of Tio Pepe we shared in Paris, we were friends, and she trusted me not to share the news and opinions she confided in me.

In one of her letters, Mavis remarked that she had imagined I was expecting another baby. I was startled to read this, for it just so happened that I did indeed think I might be pregnant again, and I had not planned on a fourth child. How had she guessed?

One of my few regrets, where Mavis is concerned, is that I didn't tell her how uncannily perceptive this remark was. It was a clear indication that she was thinking about me, and I should have found a way of acknowledging that.

I had my own obstetrical thoughts about Mavis, as well, for I had started to imagine she had been pregnant sometime close to my year of birth. Against all reason, in other words, I started thinking of myself as the child she might have had.

Impossible to tell Mavis this. We weren't such intimate friends, and it would surely be impertinent for me to comment on what I imagined of her obstetrical history. By the time I replied to the letter in which she suggested I might be expecting again, I knew I was not pregnant, after all, and I never said a word about her perceptiveness—or about my conjectures.

We continued to write and to see each other whenever it was possible, in Montreal, in Toronto, in Paris, and, a few years before her death, at Symphony Space in New York City.

CONFIDENT AS I seemed to my students and colleagues, I had never lost the timidity of my adolescence—or my anxiety on the telephone. The idea of calling up a stranger like novelist and playwright George Szanto, say, and presenting myself to him as a researcher who wished to interview him about his work was daunting. Getting past that kind of anxiety took several interviews and many months, but necessity is an excellent teacher, and I eventually got to the point where I could set up an interview with equanimity.

The greater exposure I got from my research resulted in new opportunities, as well. In 1988, when I was writing the report on my research, I was invited to take over a moribund literary magazine based in Lennoxville, Quebec. So *Matrix* moved to Montreal, and a few John Abbott colleagues and I breathed new life into the magazine and made a splash across Canada. The editor of *Canadian Fiction Magazine*, Geoff Hancock, invited me to edit a special issue of the magazine on Quebec's English-language writers that became my first book when Véhicule Press published it as *Telling Differences: New English Fiction from Quebec* in 1988.[22] Publisher Simon Dardick invited me to edit a fiction series for Véhicule, to which I agreed. The Toronto publisher ECW Press invited me to write a monograph on Hugh MacLennan's novel *Two Solitudes,* as well, and that appeared in 1990.[23]

By which time I was living in Budapest.

In the Swim

I was a writer by the time my book on *Two Solitudes* came out, but I didn't feel like a writer. This was a book, yes, a hardcover book, even, but it was part of a series of monographs on classic works of Canadian fiction. All were short, and all used the same format, with the result that it seemed to me a workaday book. I was convinced that being a writer was on a loftier plane. Being a writer meant writing a novel.

I longed to be able to call myself a writer, though I still couldn't see how that would ever happen. I'd never managed to write any imaginative work other than poems abandoned long ago and short stories I had soon given up on. If I were a writer, I thought, my life would be so different. I'd be so proud of myself I'd strut around with a smile on my face all the time. I'd have made it to Mount Olympus.

It's such a romantic idea of writing, not even that unusual at the time. This was long before we started giving non-fiction writing its due, long before we started talking about "creative non-fiction" and "literary non-fiction." Long before we thought it possible to be a writer who is also a translator, a publisher, an editor, or even a festival director.

Toni Morrison, a literary goddess if ever there was one, had a prolific and varied career as editor, educator, and writer. "I know it seems like a lot," she told *New Yorker* writer Hilton Als for a profile first printed in 2003, "but I only do one thing. I read books. I teach books. I write books. I think about books. It's one job."[24]

We all have favourite writers, and I make a passionate case for the writers I admire every chance I get. I will never be a Gallant, a Lessing, or a Spark, and I'm not sure I would want to be any one of them. I know more than I once did about being a writer, about writers' lives, and especially the lives of women writers.

I also know more about myself and about what matters to me. An only child, Mavis had no family, as her father and grandmother had died when she was a girl, and she was estranged from her mother. Though married for a short time to the musician Johnny Gallant, she spent most of her life as a single woman. I spent many years as a single woman—and a single mother—so I know both the benefits and the costs. I know, too, that that was not the only life for me.

Calamities aside, I have been happy with my own life. And yes, I certainly wanted to be a writer, but not to the exclusion of all else.

MY THREE-YEAR GRANT in the 1980s paved the way for me to become a writer. It demystified the literary world and gave me the opportunity to get to know many writers who were not doing much strutting around.

Anything but. The writers I met were struggling. Struggling to balance whatever work they did to pay the rent with the writing they did because that's what they really wanted to do. Struggling to get their work published. Struggling, in many cases, to believe in themselves as writers even after they had published several books.

Interviewing these writers allowed me to understand where their work came from, too, the challenges they faced, the impact of the unique historical and political circumstances in which they were working—and the discouragement they felt in what I soon realized was a thoroughly demoralized literary milieu.

There were a few exceptions—writers who were doing well enough, usually because of good connections in U.S. or British publishing circles—but most of the writers I met were cut off from one another, cut off from the lively English-Canadian publishing scene in Toronto, cut off from the equally lively francophone literary milieu here in Quebec, and cut off from whatever readers they might have.

Those interviews, in short, opened up a world I wanted to be part of. All I had to do was walk in.

THE PARLOUS STATE of this literary community might have given me pause. Why would I want to be part of a milieu as depressed as the one I was exploring? If I had been serious only about making it as a writer, and only about furthering my literary career, I might have upped stakes and moved back to London, or at least to Toronto.

I wasn't about to do that. There was Andy and his career. Our children and their schooling. There was the fact that I felt at home in Montreal, where I had put down roots after so many years of moving from place to place. I was neither single-minded enough nor foolish enough to give that all up. No way.

It was all very well to know I just had to walk in; that didn't mean it was easy. I couldn't write, at least I couldn't write fiction. By the time I went back to teaching, in 1988, I was so busy with my job, my family, my research, and these new publishing opportunities that there was next to no time left over for writing fiction, and there was no space in my mind for anything other than the next appointment, the next class, the next deadline, and the next meal.

SO, THERE I was, on the point of understanding the difficulties of being a writer working in a minority community. Knowing that few were interested in their work, even when they did manage to get it published. Knowing that even fewer were interested in what I had been learning about them. Knowing enough, in other words, to know this was a crazy place to create a literary career. And instead of being put off, I was hooked.

What I saw in this demoralized literary community was an opportunity. An opportunity to get involved. To pitch in and do something. To write about some of these writers and their work. More than that I did not know, but that was the start.

The timing was propitious. I was far from the only person aware of the predicament of the Anglo literary community. There was a move to create an organization called QSPELL—the Quebec Society for the Promotion of English-Language Literature—to celebrate the best books published by writers working here in English.

I took an active role in that, getting my first taste of the political obstacles writers faced.

What I did was for my own good, certainly, for I was starting to make my mark. What I did was for the good of the community, too. I loved, and I still love, working with others—publishers, librarians, booksellers, journalists, producers, writers, translators, readers—for the common good.

I was ambitious, certainly, but not only for myself. I was ambitious for myself as part of the community I was getting to know.

AND NO SOONER had I found a foothold in this literary world than I took a giant step out of it—and into a different world entirely.

By the time my three-year grant ended, we had sold our house on Golf Avenue and moved into a large stone bungalow on the Lakeshore Road. I had written up my research and edited the collection of Anglo stories that Véhicule Press published in 1989. Late that year, I finished writing the essay on *Two Solitudes* that was published in 1990. My *Matrix* colleagues and I had successfully relaunched the magazine. And I had successfully applied for a grant to work on a new research project, too, this time on contemporary Northern Irish fiction. I would be on paid leave again, until 1992.

Andy, for his part, was due for a sabbatical year. Excited by the fall of the Berlin Wall in late 1989 and by the unexpected opening up of Eastern Europe, he wanted to spend the year in Hungary. Listening to him, I glimpsed an opportunity for myself, as well. We decided to uproot ourselves and move to Budapest.

WHAT I LOVED most about my literary life in those years was *Matrix* magazine, which became the closest thing to a salon I had ever known. How could I leave that behind? This would be my one regret as I got ready to leave Montreal, and that's how I knew I'd be back.

A month before we left for Budapest, I threw a party to bring everyone I'd been working with together under one roof—the other editors, the designer, a dozen or more contributors.

Patrick Coleman, a former Montrealer teaching at UCLA and a star reviewer for *Matrix*, was at that party along with his wife, Susan. He had read but never met the Slovenian-Canadian essayist Tom Ložar, who wrote under the pen name A.D. Person (as in A Displaced Person) and translated poetry from Slovenian into English. Co-editor Kenneth Radu—who had recently reviewed an extraordinary book on contemporary poetry in Arabic by the Lebanese-born Montrealer John Asfour—was there with his wife, Diane Hibbard, who managed the business side of the magazine, and our wonderful art director, Susan Valyi.

Maurie Alioff, who wrote eye-opening articles on Canadian film for *Matrix*, had seen the names of other contributors in issues of the magazine and had read their stuff, but this was the first time he'd ever met them.

"This is like the French resistance," he said to me, "the Maquis. We each knew only you, and this is the first time we get to meet the others."

I laughed at the image of us as a small, secret resistance group. The difference in context from wartime France was vast, but it was true we were allies in a literary and cultural cause.

And what was that cause? There was a dearth of outlets for Quebec writers working in English, and

Matrix addressed that directly. Non-francophones having become all but invisible as Quebec nationalism took hold, *Matrix* also addressed the lack of awareness that there were writers like us in Quebec. In other words, we were creating opportunities for ourselves and other non-francophones; we wanted to show the world that we were here.

Some of my guests were writers, artists, and translators I'm still working with today. I got to know others after that party, after I returned from Budapest and moved from the magazine to writing and literary activism—and then on to Blue Metropolis and book publishing.

The initial goal was to ensure that the writers would no longer be ignored, and so we sought to create not only fresh opportunities but a more inclusive Quebec—and a more inclusive Canada. New people joined in, others went on their way and disappeared, sometimes forever, and some of them then came back into view years or decades later, wearing the same old hat, or a different one.

Peripatetic though my early life had been, this evolving literary salon has provided me with a deep sense of continuity. It has been the source of abiding friendship, professional support, intellectual stimulation, fun, and a sense of community that is centred in Montreal though never limited to Montreal.

I didn't think of *Matrix* as a salon at the time, but that is what it was. I had started as a teenager with *The Trojan Women,* helping to direct as well as playing one of the major onstage parts. I had been devoting a lot of time to others—to my family, first and foremost, to my students, to the writers I had met, and to literary causes. Solitary as I often need to be, I also love being part of something bigger than myself—part of a world in which I belong and to which I can contribute. And though there were armies of detractors, as there always are when a community starts to mobilize, there was an exciting sense of possibility, as well. Something not entirely unlike the whiff of change that Mavis had found so exciting in the Montreal of the 1940s.[25]

I WASN'T A wealthy intellectual facing off against Napoleon from her château on Lake Geneva. Far from. This was a different cultural context entirely from that of Madame de Staël. I wasn't elaborately coiffed and dressed, the glasses we served wine from were not exquisite, and I'd prepared the food myself.

There was no comparison with the world in which Staël had moved in post-revolutionary France, and yet these people milling about that stone bungalow on the Lakeshore Road were writers and translators, artists and intellectuals. They were glad to exclaim when they could put a face to a name they knew, and to chat with new acquaintances about their last piece, what they were working on now, and what they were planning.

Which is how it happened that I realized one of my dreams in 1990, on the eve of our departure for Budapest, where I would soon realize the other.

5.
The
Girl
from
Dream
City

C'est une ville de rêve.
—PIERRE BOURQUE, 2001

Budapest

It was a reckless decision, to uproot us all and move to Hungary. There was suddenly so much to do, in addition to all the usual end-of-semester marking. So much stress, as well. I had to plan for my Irish research project, buy my first laptop computer and a portable printer, take a course on word processing, prepare a new issue of *Matrix* for the press, ask my nonplussed associates to play a bigger role keeping the magazine going in my absence, and meet with the heads of my sons' schools. We were negotiating with a real estate agent to sell a parcel of land on the other side of the Lakeshore Road, too. And then we turned around and spent the money on a Volkswagen Westphalia camper van that we would pick up in Europe.

And we found tenants for our house, except that these turned out to be tenants who didn't pay the rent. We did get rid of them, though that took some doing, long-distance from Budapest. Our real estate agent found us a new tenant, whom we had never met, and we soon learned he was a disbarred lawyer with a history of taking over people's houses and defrauding them. So, in addition to the loss of yet more revenue, we also incurred legal expenses in the year-long process of getting this crook to move out of our house.

We were thriving in Europe, however, and somehow—we must have been mad—we convinced ourselves to prolong our stay in Hungary for a second year. It was only on our return to Montreal, in the summer of 1992, that we discovered that the crooked tenant had stolen our belongings and vandalized our house.

So, the decision to move to Hungary was not only expensive and in some ways crazy, but also disastrous.

It was also the best decision ever, at least for me. If *Matrix* was the unexpected realization of one dream, Budapest became the realization of another. What made Madame de Staël the *grande dame* I admired was not only her salon, her artistic and intellectual friends, and her willingness to joust with Napoleon; it was also the fact that she herself was a writer.

It was in Budapest that I became a writer.

ANDY AND I had stayed in touch with our dissident friends, but there was no way of knowing what to expect in 1990, now that the political winds had changed so dramatically. Budapest had fascinated me from the start, and I relished the opportunity to get to know it better. I wouldn't be teaching, so I knew I'd have more time in Budapest than I would ever have in Montreal; at that juncture, time is what I needed most.

I knew, too, that I would be in a privileged position to witness whatever changes there would be in Hungarian society. I would write about those changes, I thought.

I would keep a journal and turn some of that into an essay I might be able to publish.

IT DIDN'T WORK out like that. I did keep a journal, and I also wrote long letters to friends and family with many of the details of everyday life in Hungary, describing the street we lived on, and quoting our landlady, newly elected politicians, and the woman who sold hot peppers at the market. We were spending time with old friends and making new ones, not only politicians but actors, filmmakers, philosophers, writers, musicians, and artists.

I got to know my way around the city, and Budapest was soon the favourite of all the cities I had known, usurping the role that Paris had held since I was twenty, overtaking even Manhattan. I loved Budapest's coffee houses and its elegant, run-down apartment buildings, its outdoor markets, its art deco architecture, and the Liszt Ferenc Academy of Music, which is the most beautiful of all the concert halls I have seen.

I worked long-distance on material for the next issue of *Matrix*, I wrestled with a problematical translation I was editing for Véhicule Press, and I travelled to Northern Ireland for my new research project. I spent time in the Linen Hall Library in Belfast—the library from which Granny Jo used to borrow books by the great Russians. And from Belfast I travelled up the Antrim coast to St. MacNissi's College for a summer school on Northern Irish writers of the 1930s and 1940s.

The Giant's Causeway

The summer school had attracted me both for professional and for personal reasons. My research was focused on contemporary fiction written by Northern Irish writers, not on that older generation, but I wanted to understand the context out of which the contemporary writing had emerged. The summer school program included figures I was interested in, especially the great Irish critic Edna Longley, who had recently published a stimulating pamphlet on the intersection where Irish literary culture met hunger strikers and nationalism.[26]

I wanted to learn about the world into which my parents had come of age in the 1930s and 1940s, and I wanted to find out about some of the writers and broadcasters—Sam Hanna Bell, John Stewart, Bertie Rodgers, Louis MacNeice—who had been their friends and associates.

I learned more than I had expected, about Sam Hanna Bell especially, whose fiction was impressive. There were many social exchanges, as well, for there were about a hundred participants in the summer school, and we ate together at long tables in the refectory.

THE MOST SIGNIFICANT exchange I had was with a woman called Harriet Armstrong, who came up to me to introduce herself.

She must have inquired of the organizers of the summer school who I was, for she had a purpose in coming over to chat with me. She was from Lisburn, she said, and she asked about my family. When I mentioned that my father had been a doctor in Lisburn in the late 1940s and early 1950s, she said, "I think your father brought me into the world."

I stared at her in disbelief, but she was serious. She had spoken without hesitation, too. She must have known as soon as she learned my name and knew I'd lived in Lisburn as a child.

"When would that have been?" I asked.

The dates were right; she was my age, born in Lisburn.

"My mother always talked about young Dr. Leith," she told me. "She always said he was such a gentle doctor."

Her words were a gift to me, more than a gift. The man her mother had described was not the father I had known. The father I knew was not gentle, not with me. He was a charming, complicated man, controlling and tyrannical and unstable. Oh, he must have been able to function well, even brilliantly, in his working life; he was a successful man, until he wasn't.

But gentle? That cast a new light on Desmond.

It was six years since he had died, and I still regretted that I had so seldom had a conversation with him.

Was I suffering from delayed homesickness for my home in earliest childhood—a home I never knew I'd had? Was I grieving for the idealistic young doctor my father had once been?

Not quite. What I felt now was something quite different. Not forgiveness. Something far more complicated than that. Regret and ambivalence, yes. And something new, as well. Something that changed everything.

My father is remembered in Lisburn as a gentle doctor. How could that be? How could I not have known that he was gentle? Harriet had made me cry, yes, but she had done far more than that. She had changed my thinking.

I didn't know what to make of what she had told me. All I knew was that it contradicted everything my own experience had taught me.

I searched my memory. Yes, there had been those stories he read to us. Yes, he had taken my brothers and me to Lord's Cricket Ground once for a match. He had taken me to the Royal Albert Hall for the Last Night of the Proms. And yes, he had written lovingly to his parents, a few years before they died within days of each other. I knew this because Sheelagh had sent me a copy of a letter from Basel that had been found among family papers. Reading it, I recognized Daddy's assertive handwriting at once, but not the sweetness in his voice.

Harriet Armstrong was moving me closer to a new understanding of my father.

I wasn't there yet. There was something I still didn't know, there had to be. Something that would make sense of what Harriet had said. It must be something that had changed after 1949, which was when Harriet had been born.

It had changed in the 1950s, while we were living at Haddon Hall, and it was my mother, in her old age, who would let me in on the secret in her kitchen in Canterbury.

THE PAST DOESN'T drift back into focus, not when it's a past that had always seemed too dramatic for words. It lurches back into the foreground in fits and starts, galvanized by a chance meeting with a woman my father brought into the world—and by a mesmerizing television series I happened to see a few years after my stay on the Antrim coast.

Watching television one evening in the 1990s, I caught the start of a series called *Doctor Finlay*. There was something familiar about the name, and something familiar about the Scottish town where he lived, too. It was a remake, I realized.

I watched, mesmerized, immersed partly in this Scottish Television series, which I had never seen before, and partly in *Dr. Finlay's Casebook*, the old BBC series I had watched with my parents in London in the early 1960s.

I remembered the silence that had fallen over my parents while they were watching that. And that almost forgotten time when my father, too, was a country doctor.

I had forgotten all about Dr. Finlay until this new series caught my attention. I studied the closing credits when the episode of the Scottish Television series ended, and that's how I discovered there was a book about Dr. Finlay—and, coincidentally, about the kind of life we ourselves had led in Lisburn. Both television series were based on *Country Doctor,* by A.J. Cronin, a Scottish writer who had himself been a doctor.[27]

It's quite possible that my father read *Country Doctor* in Northern Ireland. He certainly knew about Dr. Cronin. Daddy had revered the Scottish author ever since he was a young doctor and read Cronin's novel *The Citadel,* the sensationally successful work about medical practice in a Welsh mining village that paved the way for the National Health Service.

Dr. Cronin was a ghostly presence in my parents' lives, all our lives. They had had no reason to mention him to me, when we were watching television together, and I hadn't known enough to be curious about him when I was twelve years old.

Except that I was curious. Enforced passivity has some obvious disadvantages, especially when I was getting pummelled in the school playground. It has a few advantages, as well, at least for a writer. I was a good observer.

SO, I DID some research on Dr. Cronin, learning that he had been on staff at Tredegar Cottage Hospital in Wales in the early 1920s. Also on staff, I discovered, and at the very same time, was Aneurin Bevan.

Dr. Bevan is the Welsh doctor who became minister of health in the postwar Labour government that brought in the NHS in 1948—and who resigned when the House of Commons cut all coverage of vision care. As a child, I had been marked by my father's stories of that great debate—and of his boundless admiration for Aneurin Bevan. As an adolescent in Canada, I had heard Daddy rail against conditions in the Welsh mines, too. And now, as a woman of forty, I could see how the experiences of Dr. Cronin and Dr. Bevan in Wales fit together with my own parents' experience in Lisburn, Northern Ireland.

Fascinating as I found this connection, it didn't actually help me process what I had learned from Harriet Armstrong on the Antrim coast. That would take longer.

I WAS LINING up for breakfast at St. MacNissi's when I got into conversation with a student named Jenny.

"So where are you from?" she asked.

"I'm from here," I responded. This was something I never got to say, so I relished the moment. It was disingenuous, though, as it was perfectly obvious to Jenny that I was not really from Northern Ireland. My accent is a giveaway everywhere I go, with too many different influences to be easily placed.

Zadie Smith writes in her essay "Speaking in Tongues" about Archibald Leach, who grew up speaking with a Bristol accent before he transformed himself into the Cary Grant who had a "heavenly sui generis accent, neither west country nor posh, American nor English." That accent came from nowhere, Smith says, "*he* came from nowhere."[28]

As *The New Yorker* movie critic Pauline Kael put it, "Ingrid Bergman doesn't sound Swedish to us but sounds simply like Ingrid Bergman. Cary Grant became stateless early: he was always Cary Grant." Kael called him "The Man from Dream City."[29]

In Canada, I sound English. In England, I sound American. When I'm in Northern Ireland, or speaking to someone from Northern Ireland—or merely talking about Northern Ireland—I sound to myself as though I never left. No one in Ireland is ever taken in. It's a rare individual anywhere who picks up on the Irish inflections. My accent comes from nowhere, like Cary Grant's. I come from nowhere.

This can pose difficulties.

"I was born in Belfast, and I live in Montreal," I told Jenny.

I should have stopped there. I should have known better than to go on.

I did know better, and I still went too far. "But I'm living in Budapest, at the moment."

I knew it was a mistake to say this.

So, why did I do it? This wasn't a border official who needed to know where I'd travelled from. This was an unsuspecting student from Belfast.

The reason I mentioned Budapest was that I was feeling the great contrast between where I now lived and where I was from. I was out of my element in Budapest, struggling with a foreign language in a foreign city, and now here I was, back in Northern Ireland, where I had been born, and a short distance from the town I'd lived in as a small child. My story, and its many changes of place, were very much on my mind during my stay on the Antrim coast.

Even today, when I've written about the different places I've lived, I rarely say much about my travels except in the company of family or close friends. It's factual, it's true, but it isn't what most people want to hear.

Jenny had no way of knowing any of this.

"That's too much for me, before breakfast," she snapped, turning away.

I HAD BECOME very good at *not* telling my story, in other words. I'd had a lifetime of practice at that. There were people I'd known for decades who knew I'd come to Canada from England, but who weren't aware I was originally from Belfast. Most knew one or two parts of the story, but no more. If they knew I'd been to school in Basel, they didn't know I had spoken German, let alone Baslerdütsch. Many don't know I lived in Budapest or that I married a Hungarian refugee.

These were some of the fundamentals of my life, and I had kept quiet about them. I'd kept much hidden from myself, as well, having succeeded in expunging memories of a secret pleasure in the garden of Haddon Hall, of Basel, much else besides.

OF COURSE MY international background was too much for Jenny. It was too much for me, too.

I had spent decades unable to acknowledge where I came from, where I'd been, what I'd done, and who I was.

So, I'd been right all along—right to keep quiet and mete out my story in small portions, when I mentioned it at all. I'd always known my story was hard to take, and I'd got into the habit of saying nothing.

NOT THAT DIFFERENT, really, from those moments when Andy arrived home with unexpected guests. I would look at him in dismay, but I never said, "I can't stand it when you just show up with unexpected guests!" Not to him and not to whoever was with him.

I cast my eyes over those faces and could see how happy they were to be on our doorstep, how delighted they were at the prospect of a dinner or a party. None of this was their fault. I welcomed them to my home.

Saying nothing was not a good strategy. It gave Andy permission to pull the same stunt again, a week or a month later. I did complain to him when our guests had gone on their way, but he never took that seriously.

I COULD HAVE come up with some plausible story in the breakfast queue at St. MacNissi's College, something that would have irked Jenny less.

I could surely have done a better job now than I had, in high school, when I pretended I'd gone curling over the weekend.

Yes, I was from here, originally, I could say. And then I could have added, "I live in Galway."

Imagine how that conversation might go.

Jenny smiles and tells me about the cousin who is a schoolteacher in Galway.

"I have a cousin not far from here," I say—this is the truth, and it's always a good idea to include a dollop of truth to lend credence to the entirely fanciful.

Jonathan Swift knew that when he described Gulliver's third voyage to Laputa, Balnibarbi, Luggnagg, and Japan. Swift had been on my mind, too; on my way north to St. MacNissi's, I'd come through Kilroot, where he had lived as a young man.

(I should add that it's good to add something fanciful to the earnestly truthful, too.)

"Whereabouts would that be?" Jenny asks.

"On Strangford Lough," I say. "He built a house for his family on Strangford Lough."

This is within the bounds of the world Jenny is familiar with, and it happens to be true. Like his father, Raymond, my cousin Julian is an architect, and that's where he built his house.

"Right," she says. She nods to herself, sets her Ulster fry on her tray, and moves over to the coffee urn.

"Did you ever see the film *December Bride*?" I ask, following in her footsteps. This is the finest film I've ever seen about Northern Ireland, and it's based on a novel by Sam Hanna Bell.

She perks up. "I did that."

"*December Bride* was filmed close to my cousin's house." This, too, is the unsullied truth.

"Was it, indeed?"

She smiles. We pick up our trays and sit down together to eat.

THERE IS SUCH a thing as too much truth. The broad strokes of my life sound glamorous, and there's no doubt I have been fortunate in many ways. The problem in talking about the places I've lived is that it sounds like bragging.

That was one reason to keep myself to myself, that the mere mention of those foreign cities sounds boastful. That's what I thought, anyway, though it might have been truer to say I was modest to a fault.

I could have said more, in a friendly, chatty way. Some people are good at that, at just being friendly and chatty. I could have explained what I knew about how we happened to move to Basel, say. That wasn't glamorous at all, but I'd been told never to talk about the Communist Party, so it was just as well I'd all but forgotten about that.

I didn't want to brag, and I didn't want the person I was with to feel bad because they had never had an opportunity to live in Basel, or Montreal, or Budapest. It was too long a story, anyway—how it happened, why it happened—and I only knew the half of it. Besides, I was always more comfortable keeping myself to myself.

SO WHY HAD I broken the habit of a lifetime and said more to Jenny?

Being back in Northern Ireland was certainly part of it, especially as this was the morning after the conversation I'd had with Harriet Armstrong about my father's gentle bedside manner.

But there was more to it than that. This was part of the bigger change I was living through. Providing too much information to Jenny was one of the earliest signs of a change in the way I present myself to others.

Desmond had always warned me to keep quiet, and I had done as he wished. His death had been devastating, and I had still not recovered. "A star too blinding to look at straight on," Dany Laferrière writes. "That's what a dead father is."[30]

But my father's death was also a liberation. By the time I did recover, I had become a different person.

It takes time to change the habits of a lifetime. My father had been dead almost six years by the time I moved to Budapest, and I was just beginning to come to terms with the jaguar he had been—and with the life I wanted for myself. And now here I was, back in Northern Ireland—and Harriet Armstrong had turned him into a pussycat.

THAT STAY IN Northern Ireland contributed to an upheaval I was not conscious of at the time. I didn't yet know how the story would turn out, and I had no idea how to tell it. Poor Jenny had just happened to be next to me that morning when I started in on it so clumsily.

She avoided me for the rest of the week, and I can't blame her.

Birds of Passage

I returned to Budapest laden with the books I had bought in Northern Ireland and set about reading them. It was September, and my sons were starting school next door to the villa where we lived. Andy had set up an office downtown and was busy with his consulting work.

I took a Hungarian language class and shopped at the Moscow Square market. I took Hector for walks over the Hill of Roses. I made breakfast, lunch—the boys all came home for lunch—and dinner. I met my sons' school friends and entertained them with my comically flawed Hungarian. I chatted as well as I could with our landlady and her sister, who lived downstairs with their families. I edited manuscripts for *Matrix* and for Véhicule Press. And I wrote about what I was observing of life in post-Communist Budapest.

In October, a political crisis over the price of gasoline added intensity and drama to the scenes I was writing. And then something remarkable happened. I moved from recording scraps of what the landlady and the market woman said to creating characters and writing dialogue. I created an imaginary family of Canadians caught up in a political crisis in Budapest. I developed these scenes and turned them into a story.

I celebrated my fortieth birthday in December, and then we drove across northern Europe from Budapest to Canterbury to spend Christmas with my family. We took the long way back in January, stopping in southern France and Italy, before getting back to Budapest, where I continued writing all winter long, all spring. I was imagining a world not unlike the one I was living in but entirely my own.

I knew this was it. This is what I'd always wanted to do, sit at my desk and write. I didn't want to stop, which is why I readily agreed when Andy suggested we stay on for a second year in Budapest; I was sure I would never be able to finish what I was working on in Montreal.

By the summer of 1991, I had the first draft of a novel. I sent one copy to Brian, another to a writer friend, and I got helpful comments back that allowed me to see what I'd done and what I still needed to do. One useful suggestion was that I should provide my characters with bodies—and it was true that I'd entirely forgotten to comment on their appearance. Brian also recommended Dorothea Brande's classic guide to creative writing, *Becoming a Writer,* which I found invaluable.

I worked on the novel again the following year, developing the characters, describing them, and expanding the story, which is about the passage from one place to another, politically, geographically, or emotionally. A story about change, in other words. The first of many stories I have told about change, I realize as I write this.

So, it was in Budapest that I found gold in the streets. I was living a version of the bohemian life I had dreamed of when I was starting out in 1970. By the time my family and I went home to our ruined house in Pointe-Claire, I had the manuscript of a novel in my suitcase. It was called *Birds of Passage*.

AND I STILL couldn't think of myself as a writer. I'd published the book on *Two Solitudes*, but I didn't think that counted as real writing, and I'd now finished a second draft of a novel. It still wasn't enough, not for me. I had to find a publisher for the novel. Only then would I be able to call myself a writer.

I met publisher Karen Haughian at a literary event in Montreal a couple of months later and mentioned that I'd written a novel. She asked to see it, liked it, and published it the following spring.

SO, WHAT HAD happened here? What had made it possible for me to become a writer, at long last?

Time, for a start. I had more time and fewer stresses than I had had since I was a student. Inspiration played a role, too, for I felt inspired in Budapest as I had never felt inspired before. I was on the cusp of glimpsing the new life that would take the place of the life I had been leading.

Those encounters at St. MacNissi's College on the Antrim coast had something to do with this.

Speaking Hungarian had a lot to do with it, too. My immersion in such a foreign language—Hungarian is not an Indo-European language, but one of the small number of Finno-Ugrian languages—and its foreign idiom had revitalized my thinking, too, in more ways than I could articulate.

It wasn't just time, though, or inspiration. There was a bowl of soup, too, and that comes under another heading altogether.

ANDY AND I were with our sons in a restaurant on the Corso one afternoon after I returned to Budapest from Northern Ireland. I ordered a bowl of *sóskaleves*, not knowing what kind of soup it was. I loved other Hungarian soups and had no doubt I would love this, too.

The menu was in Hungarian, with no translation to German or English, and I'd never come across *sóskaleves* before. "*Leves*" was easy, for "*leves*" means soup, but neither Andy nor the waiter was able to tell me what "*sóska*" was in English.

I took a spoonful. A slightly sweet, subtle flavour with a tart edge, almost like—what? It tasted something like wild strawberries. Or rosehips.

I knew that flavour, but what was it?

I took another spoonful, and something shifted in my little world.

What I was tasting in that soup was a flavour I had known, once upon a time.

I reached back in time, far back, trying to identify when I'd tasted this flavour before.

When was that? Where had I been?

IT WAS IN Beckenham. Yes. It was that leafy plant I'd discovered in our garden at Haddon Hall. I'd been five years old, and I had eaten those leaves with a pleasure that was both pure and illicit.

I'd never told my mother about it. I'd never mentioned it to anyone. And I'd never tasted it since, not once. I had forgotten all about it—about the discovery, the secrecy, the pleasure, and the joy of a pleasure that was mine alone.

In that moment in Budapest, beside the Danube, the deliciousness of my childhood transgression flooded back into my consciousness. I was five years old again, nibbling this appealing herb. Loving what I knew was not allowed.

IT WAS A madeleine moment, to be sure—but it was more than that, too. This was a Proustian moment with a linguistic twist.

Budapest was foreign, of course, and perhaps it was the city's foreignness that reminded me of Basel. I was now learning Hungarian, but I communicated with some of Andy's older relatives in a mix of Hungarian and such German as I could reconstruct. The physical details in Budapest—the streetcars, the metal grates around the oak trees, the design of door knobs, the wooden shutters—were stirring up memories of the equally foreign city I'd known as a child.

My long-lost friend Madeleine from Basel was somewhere in the picture, too, conjured up like Princess Leia by the crazy coincidence of her name—for she really was called Madeleine, Madeleine Tripet, I'm not making this up—and that of Proust's *petite madeleine*.

The individual is a succession of individuals, Beckett wrote in his thesis on Proust, and the periods of transition from one to another "represent the perilous zones in the life of the individual, dangerous, precarious, painful, mysterious and fertile."[31] It is the action of involuntary

223

memory—as with that long-forgotten taste of the tea cake dipped in tisane that figures so significantly in Proust's novel—that can spark these moments of upheaval.

I was in a perilous zone in the summer of 1990. I'd left a dozen years of life in suburban Montreal behind. I was in a foreign place, living in a language I understood only sporadically. And I'd now returned to Budapest from a visit to Northern Ireland that had upended my memories of my father in ways I couldn't make sense of.

PROUST'S MARCEL HAD had no difficulty either recognizing the madeleine or knowing what to call it. Sitting in that restaurant by the Danube in 1990, I could not identify the flavour of the soup I had in front of me. I had to wait until we got back to our apartment to look up "*sóska.*"

Sorrel.

Sóska was sorrel.

The name of those leaves I'd discovered as a little girl was sorrel.

It was the taste of sorrel that had transported me back to that garden in Beckenham. And that was its moment of glory. Sorrel never had the same effect on me again.

Sorrel is seldom available at the market near where I now live, and on the rare occasions when I have eaten it in the years since that extraordinary bowl of soup— mostly in salads—I've recognized it, of course, but it has no longer had the power to astonish me as it did that afternoon in Budapest.

But then I haven't needed it to have that power. Sorrel had done its work.

Return

It was only when we arrived back in Pointe-Claire
in July 1992 that we discovered that our house had
been vandalized. Our tenant and his son had sold
most of our belongings and trashed most of the rest,
going so far as to puncture cans of sardines and leave
them to rot in our kitchen cupboards.

Andy went back to Hungary a month later and spent
much of the next twenty years dividing his time between
Montreal and Budapest. Before he left, he had arranged
for an alarm system to be installed. We were still married,
but only just. Our sons were aged fifteen, thirteen, and
nine, and I was now effectively a single mother.

It wasn't the toughest time in my life, but it was a
calamity. A double whammy, in fact. The state of our
house and the state of my marriage. It was easier by far
to think about the house.

I rarely burst into tears, but that's what I did on my
first day back at John Abbott College, when a friendly
colleague asked about the house. I burst into tears again,

a few weeks later, when I saw a book inscribed to me by the author—and stolen from our house—for sale in a second-hand bookshop.

I found it almost impossible to talk about what had happened to the house, at first. I was then surprised to learn that it was good for me to do so. It was in the process of talking about it that I discovered how dramatic the story is.

People wanted to know, who was this guy?

"He's a disbarred lawyer, and he was living in the house with his son. It was the son, apparently, who was responsible for the sardine cans."

Whatever possessed them to do this?

"They've done it before, with other people's houses. He's a man journalists describe as 'well-known to the police.'"

And he's never been caught?

"It can be very helpful to know the law. He has been very successful at evading and avoiding charges. He got away unscathed when someone tossed a firebomb into one of the houses he had trashed."

Did your neighbours know him?

"Not so far as I am aware. He did manage to sidle up to our own lawyer, who lives nearby."

There were big gaps in what I knew about this crook, whom I never met and never wanted to meet. But somehow, in the midst of the difficulties of the time, I found my imagination filling in the gaps.

IT IS UNTRUE to say that dire circumstances and experiences are the meat of fiction, although they can play a starring role. *The Tragedy Queen* came into being in the wake of our catastrophic homecoming, and it would not be the novel it is if it hadn't been for that crook and his son. What was—and remained—a source of personal anguish was also an opportunity for me as a writer.

I have survived. We replaced some of the items that had been trashed or stolen. I continued to live in the house with the boys and with Andy, when he was in town, and eventually found an opportunity to leave the suburbs, and move into Montreal. Andy and I had drifted apart, and our dreams were set in different cities—his in Budapest, mine in Montreal. After several years of living in limbo, mostly apart, sometimes together, we got divorced.

WORK IS ONE remedy for sorrow, and good company is another. A ragtag band of like-minded spirits had got together while I was away, and they invited me to join them to create a writers' organization that became the Federation of English-language Writers of Quebec. To our surprise, this new organization promptly became the beneficiary of provincial funding when the Quebec government decided to fund Anglo publishers', playwrights', and writers' associations.

At the wise suggestion of my friend and co-conspirator Ann Charney, we soon set about merging this new writers' organization with QSPELL. The result was the creation of the Quebec Writers' Federation, which soon became the cornerstone of our literary community.

I was back at John Abbott College that fall, teaching full time, and I was still publishing *Matrix* and editing manuscripts for Véhicule Press. I had started work on my second novel, *The Tragedy Queen*, which is about a tenant from hell in Pointe-Claire village, and I was working with Karen, my publisher, on the final edits of *Birds of Passage*.

Birds of Passage appeared in the spring of 1993, and I sent a copy to Mavis, who responded that I was starting late, but said I was a talented writer.

KAREN HAD BEEN coaching me on how to prepare for a reading, an interview, and other novelties, but I still found the sudden spotlight on my writing unnerving. Acknowledging that I was a writer meant facing up to the ways I had been changing—and facing up to the change in how others viewed me, as well.

Coming out as a writer forced me, in other words, to come out as the person I really am. Which would have been fine, except that it was also giving me a new reason for keeping quiet. There are some who will hate me for this, I thought. For this, too.

And yes, there were some who did.

THE EARLY 1990S were the years leading up to the second referendum on the independence of Quebec, which took place on October 30, 1995. The *indépendantiste* side lost by a hair, a result that left Quebec divided. It didn't help that Premier Jacques Parizeau blamed the referendum loss on "money and the ethnic vote."

I read an editorial in the influential nationalist newspaper *Le Devoir* in the winter of 1996 with great interest. Focusing on the open-minded younger generation of English-speaking artists and intellectuals in Quebec, the newspaper's publisher Lise Bissonnette found reason to hope for the future. Her editorial had a galvanizing effect on me.

Elected as Quebec rep and then as second vice-chair of The Writers' Union of Canada, I started meeting with

Ann and another associate, Mary Soderstrom, to plan a literary event that would take place in French and in English and, we hoped, be organized jointly by TWUC and the Union des écrivaines et des écrivains québécois (UNEQ). In fact, the three of us organized the event ourselves, with little involvement from either of the national writers' organizations.

We set about raising money from the Conseil des arts et des lettres du Québec—but we had to do this in our own names and open a personal bank account in order to deposit the funds and pay the costs of renting the hall—the Lion d'Or—and the participants' honoraria.

One of UNEQ's welcome contributions was that a junior employee came up with the name for our event, Write pour écrire, which took place on Halloween night, 1996, a year almost to the day after that divisive referendum. We were flabbergasted not only by the capacity crowd, but also by its diversity—an unprecedented mix of Montreal francophones, anglophones, and allophones. The show itself was professional and impressive, with writers reading from one another's work in translation, accompanying music, and host Winston McQuade, who speaks English and French with equal ease.

Blue Metropolis

There was already a literary festival in Montreal—the Festival de la littérature[32]— and it provided a showcase for francophone writers from Quebec and elsewhere. It was the success of Write pour écrire that convinced me there was a place in Montreal for an international literary festival that would take place in more than one language. That festival became Blue Metropolis.

It was a long road from idea to realization, though, and there was opposition from some nationalist writers and intellectuals to the idea of an international literary festival that would include not only French but English, as well—and soon other Montreal languages. This is a story I have told before, and anyone interested in how Blue Metropolis came to be may be interested in my book *Writing in the Time of Nationalism.*

This book you are reading now is more personal, however, and such an undertaking could not fail to have a massive impact on me. I worked full tilt on Blue Met for fifteen years, including the eighteen months it took to get the festival up and running. Launched in late April 1999, Blue Metropolis soon became one of the biggest and by far the most diverse of Canadian literary festivals. I had resigned from John Abbott College, too, unable to both teach and run the festival, so I was suffering from an excess of uncertainty and anxiety as well as a tidal wave of work.

Blue Metropolis brought together writers from every community and from every corner of the world. As hoped, it allowed Montreal writers working in English to bypass Toronto and go straight to the wider world. It brought together so many of the loves of my life— my love of books, of the literary salon, of writers and writing, of performance, of translation, of language and of languages. My love for bringing people together, too. Of creating something new. Of rolling up my sleeves and getting on with it. Of doing good in the world.

PAULINE KAEL, IN *The New Yorker*, is the one who describes Cary Grant as "The Man from Dream City," but Zadie Smith is the one who tries to describe such a city.

"I haven't described Dream City," she writes in "Speaking in Tongues." "I'll try to. It is a place of many voices, where the unified singular self is an illusion. . . . In Dream City everything is doubled, everything is various. You have no choice but to cross borders and speak in tongues."[33]

I'm a citizen of Dream City, too, like Zadie Smith, like countless others.

Half the world is from Dream City. And Dream City is not only where we're from. It's where we're headed, too. I can't speak for what Pauline Kael saw in Cary Grant, but in Zadie Smith's "Speaking in Tongues," the place of many voices, where everything is various, lies in the future, not in the past.

The mayor of Montreal in the early days of Blue Metropolis was Pierre Bourque, and he participated in the opening ceremony of the third festival, in April 2001. Like everyone else, he was curious about the name, about where the name came from, so I told him that Blue Metropolis is a city, first and foremost, a city inspired by Fritz Lang's great film *Metropolis*.

I told him how I'd read the philosophical novel *On Being Blue* and loved the multiplicity of meanings of "blue" that author William H. Gass conjures up in the opening pages of that book.[34]

Blue Metropolis is a utopian idea, I told Mayor Bourque, a city of many different languages and communities and peoples, a city of diversity, of multiplicity. It's the city we want to live in.

Mayor Bourque nodded. "*C'est une ville de rêve*," he said.

A dream city.

LITERARY FESTIVALS HAVE an unfortunate habit of inviting many of the same writers, so that the same big names travel from city to city in any given literary season to appear in a whole series of festivals. Some artistic directors plan a series of events that are interchangeable with those held elsewhere, except for the local hosts.

I have been to many such festivals, in which the artistic director is mostly interested in invitations to the literary stars newly published by big international publishers. This appeals to some part of the audience—and to the festival bookseller, as well, and to sponsors interested primarily in attendance figures. Such a focus on big stars is inevitable when so much depends on the bottom line, but it's a mistake.

What makes a significant literary festival is the extent to which the artistic direction of the festival is engaged with its own unique place.

One festival that greatly impressed me was the Bocas Lit Fest in Port of Spain, Trinidad, which speaks eloquently to the specificities and challenges of literary life in the Caribbean. The Winnipeg International Writers Festival does a good job of engaging with Indigenous writers and succeeds in attracting francophone writers and a francophone public to its events.

The best example may be the vast Edinburgh International Book Festival, which I attended annually. What made Edinburgh significant was not the international stars and bestselling authors who participated—although there were many of those, and I gladly went to many of their events—but its Scottishness. In their choice of Scottish writers and themes and hosts and events, festival director Faith Liddell and her successors Catherine Lockerbie and Nick Barley turned what might have been just another festival into a forum for intellectual discussion and debate on Scottish language, literature, history, identity, culture, and nationalism in the lead-up to the 2014 referendum on Scottish independence.

Blue Metropolis is a Montreal festival. It emerged out of a uniquely Montreal cultural and political context and could have come into existence in no other city. Whatever the impact of the festival on Montreal—and this is a subject that many have spoken to over the years, sometimes critically, more often in praise—its impact on me was profound.

How could it not be? Blue Metropolis was on the cutting edge of literary politics in Canada from the outset, and I was the face of Blue Metropolis. I speak French, of course, though no one ever mistakes me for a native speaker of French. I am a writer who works in English, an Anglo, and here I was, in the unique position of being the head of a multilingual literary festival in a city and a province in which French is the only official language. And in which the heads of other international events are almost all *Québécois de souche*—old-stock Quebeckers.

THERE HAS BEEN much in the past that argues for two national literatures in Canada, one English and the other French. It's still very much true today that English Canada's literary centre is Toronto, which is where most of the English-language media and many publishers are concentrated, and the francophone literary capital is Montreal, which is where most of the francophone media and publishers are based.

This dual literary identity has started to break down with increased support for literary translation, which now includes translation from languages other than English and French. A greater awareness of the diversity of Canada is also playing a role, with greater focus on writers and book industry professionals who are Black, Indigenous, people of colour, or otherwise marginalized. All this is to the good, even if most of our literature is still written, published, promoted, and read by white Canadians in either English or French.

When Blue Metropolis started up, most Canadians knew little and had read less of writers working in any language other than their own. Coming off the success of Write pour écrire, though, it seemed to me important to build bridges between francophone and English-language writers and readers—and to complicate our sense of Canadian writing with work in other languages by writers from marginalized communities.

At Blue Metropolis, the biggest and best literary salon imaginable, we invited writers working in half a dozen or more languages in any given year to address audiences not only in translation—they often appeared alongside their translators—but *in* their own language, as well. Many such events drew audiences none of us had ever seen at literary events before.

Three Afghan women poets we had brought to Montreal appeared on stage at an event that took place entirely in Dari, with an audience of about forty Dari and Farsi speakers from Afghanistan and Iran. We didn't have the considerable resources required to provide simultaneous translation or surtitles, in any case, and we were doing something more interesting, something unprecedented: bringing in audiences who speak these languages at home.

Our 2003 Grand Prix winner was Maryse Condé, from Guadeloupe, who went on to win the Alternative Nobel prize in 2018. I was criticized by several of my associates for choosing Condé, who was not a household name, and therefore unlikely to draw large crowds to the festival. I was proud to have done so.

I was delighted by the turnout, too. The onstage conversation between Condé and Dany Laferrière was an extraordinary occasion. For the first time ever, in my experience of Montreal's hitherto mostly white literary demi-monde, the room was packed with Black writers from Haiti, Guadeloupe, Jamaica, Trinidad, and St. Thomas, and with other writers of colour.

BLUE METROPOLIS IS a festival not only for writers working in French and English, but for writers working in Yiddish and Italian, Mohawk and Portuguese, Slovenian and Inuktitut and Spanish, Haitian Creole and Vietnamese and Russian and Urdu and Arabic and Farsi and Mandarin and Scots and a few dozen other Montreal languages.

These are not only Montreal languages. They are the languages of other cities, too, but not every city is a city of language in quite the same way as Montreal. Language doesn't matter in most cities in the way it matters in Montreal, where it plays a determining role in most aspects of daily life, from politics and theatrical productions to exchanges between strangers on the street, and from signs on storefronts and restaurant menus to the language that a parrot is allowed to speak in a pet shop. It's hardly surprising to find it playing a role in a literary festival.

As a non-profit organization, Blue Metropolis had a board of directors, and putting that together had meant approaching some of the people I knew and depending on them to refer me to others. As the date of the first festival neared in the winter of 1999, I hired two people to help with the work involved.

The festival was already the work of many, in other words, and I was the founder, the president, and the artistic director. There was way too much work, an insane level of stress, some excitement and—as I was about to discover—some hostility. I got most of the praise and I got the blame. Had I had a choice, this is not the way I would have chosen to become visible, but we don't always get to choose.

IT WASN'T SURPRISING to find language playing a role in a literary festival, but it certainly surprised me to find myself at the centre of a crisis. In the wake of the near-run 1995 referendum, federal authorities had spent lavish amounts of money to highlight the Canadian government's contributions to Quebec industry and culture. Gigantic Canadian flags appeared at events all over the province, which of course outraged nationalists even before irregularities were found in the awarding of contracts—and the issue turned into a full-blown scandal.

When the Blue Metropolis festival launched in 1999, some nationalists were convinced we had benefitted from the sponsorship program and that I personally was in the pay of the Department of Canadian Heritage. This was nonsense, for I wasn't earning anywhere near enough to live on, in those early years, and neither Blue Met nor I had benefitted in any way from the sponsorship program. The idea that Blue Metropolis was a federalist plot nonetheless gained traction and persuaded some Quebec writers and journalists to view the festival—and me personally—with suspicion.

Worse still, the then-president of UNEQ actively campaigned against us, doing her best to convince arts funding agencies in Quebec City and in Ottawa not to fund us. Blue Metropolis, the argument went, had embarked on a mission to undermine the French language and culture of Quebec. Not true! We had included almost sixty writers in the festival program, and more than half were francophone writers who were members of UNEQ.

It was about five weeks before our April launch date when we published the program and started publicizing that first festival. At which point, UNEQ pressed its members to cancel their participation in Blue Metropolis.

I had long known, of course, that some nationalists considered English dangerous to the future of French in Quebec, but it had not occurred to me that this could apply to a literary event. Write pour écrire had been a success, after all, even if UNEQ had been half-hearted about it. Could there really be artists and intellectuals who objected to a mix of French and English at a small, start-up literary festival?

There could.

AFTER MANY SLEEPLESS nights and anxious days, it became clear that only a handful of writers were cancelling their participation in Blue Met. Our board, sponsors, and other stakeholders stood by us, and the festival went ahead with a few last-minute substitutions.

So, there was tension, which is what you find in uncharted territory, and especially in uncharted linguistic territory in volatile Montreal. Fortunately, there were far more people who loved the idea of bringing all these different readers and writers together under one umbrella. The festival thrived.

The opposition did not end there, however, and our every move was scrutinized by nationalist intellectuals for several years. When we moved from a downtown hotel to one east of rue Saint-Denis, we were accused of moving into francophone territory. We got angry letters when a typo appeared in a French-language publicity leaflet or when an event with a francophone writer included an anglophone participant. It took the healing effects of time, some stalwart allies, and a new regime at UNEQ before Blue Metropolis was accepted.

THE EFFECT OF the crisis and its aftermath on me personally was profound. I had thought—and I continue to think—that the festival would benefit all Montreal writers, whatever their language and background, and I had not realized there could be such fervent opposition to the very idea of including English alongside French at a poetry reading or an on-stage interview. I was blindsided.

How could anyone be against building bridges? I'm from Northern Ireland. I know the formidable obstacles that have existed there, and I'm a fan of bridges. That's *why* I'm such a fan of bridges.

And how could anyone think that I would work to undermine French in Montreal? This was the last arrow I expected.

Maybe it's because the opposition to Blue Metropolis really seemed so unreasonable to me that I never got around to countering it properly. It's only now, twenty years later, that it occurs to me I could have done more to change the negative view some intellectuals had of the festival. We did publicity, of course, but I think we assumed that the value of a bilingual and multilingual festival speaks for itself. Its stellar qualities certainly seemed self-evident to me and my associates, even after it became obvious not everyone agreed. And my instinct, when under attack, was still silence.

I was little known in the francophone milieu, and I could have done more to introduce myself. I could have written a piece for *Le Devoir* about that first French course I took at McGill, about *Adolphe*, about *Les Fleurs du mal*. About the many reviews I'd written of books by Quebec writers from Marie-Claire Blais and Hubert Aquin to Jovette Marchessault. About the translation I was working on—about so much that I have written about now, in these pages, for the very first time.

It never occurred to me to write such a piece, mostly because I've only recently figured out for myself that there is a connection between different aspects of my literary life.

And if *Le Devoir*, or some other publication, had published some such piece, what difference would it have made?

I don't know the answer to that.

I did admittedly have my hands full that spring, but publishing an article along such lines never occurred to me later, either. It never occurred to my associates, at any point, though of course, I had never talked to them, or to anyone, about my life. They, too, loved the idea of building bridges, but they had no way of knowing the story I have told only now, in this book.

I WAS IN the public eye more than ever during my time at Blue Metropolis, alarmingly visible. I was also busier and more preoccupied with day-to-day activities than I had ever been.

Was festival work incompatible with writing? I was determined that it not be, but it took me a few years to learn how to carve out the time I needed to write.

The immeasurable difference between writing and most of the other activities I have spent time on is that writing is a solitary pursuit. That's what I love most about it.

Mine is not the life that novelist Bharati Mukherjee has described, growing up in Calcutta in a Brahmin household with forty or fifty other people, so that she found herself seeking refuge in hidden corners where she could read in peace. As the second of five children, though—and the eldest girl, which meant being an unpaid domestic servant—I, too, sought solitude.

My favourite sport has always been swimming, lap after solitary lap in a uncrowded pool. My favourite sound is the comfortable silence of early morning, broken only by the whisper of a page turning or the soft clicks of a keyboard. My favourite time of day is dawn, when the world seems empty, except for me. And the best refuge I found, when I was growing up, was the library—the school library, the public library, a vast reading room, any library where no one spoke.

It's not surprising that I wondered if I would ever write again during those hurly-burly years at Blue Metropolis. That's when I suggested to my publisher that I translate a short *récit autobiographique* about a Quebec author's travels in Ireland.

Voyage en Irlande avec un parapluie is a book my old friend László Rajk had mentioned to me on a visit to Montreal in the 1980s.[35] I was reminded of it when I met its author, Louis Gauthier, who was president of UNEQ in the late 1990s, just before the Blue Metropolis crisis erupted.

I lacked the emotional energy needed to write a new novel at that time, but translation, while it uses many of the same skills as writing, is less demanding. The author has done the hardest work, and the translator's job is to be true to what the author has accomplished. Translation, too, is an art, with challenges all its own, but its great advantage to me at that period was that it does not engage one's whole being as writing does. Translating Louis's book into English, I thought, would allow me to keep my hand in until I could once again work on a new book of my own.

A translation takes its own creative energy, however, and I had no energy of any kind left, by the time my Blue Metropolis day was done. The translation of even a short book takes time, too, and I had no time.

That's when I discovered the early morning. I was going to bed early, often in a state of exhaustion, and I wakened early. So, that's when I sat down to work. I'd spend an hour or two at my computer several mornings a week, and the manuscript slowly turned into *Travels with an Umbrella: An Irish Journey*.

It was a life-changing discovery, and working in the early morning has served me well ever since. When the translation was done, I started working on a new novel. After that, I was asked by writer and editor Aline Apostolska to contribute to a series of short books— Ici l'ailleurs—by Quebec writers who had lived outside of Quebec. I wrote a short first version of *Marrying Hungary* in English, Aline translated it into French, and *Épouser la Hongrie* appeared in 2004.

Travelling in northwestern China with a group that included Maggie Siggins, chair of The Writers' Union of Canada, inspired me to work on a new novel, *The Desert Lake*. I added to the original version of *Marrying Hungary*, too, and that appeared in English in 2008. The literary history *Writing in the Time of Nationalism: From Two Solitudes to Blue Metropolis* was published in December 2010.

All those books were written in the early morning, before I headed out to the office. It was like leading two lives, writing in the wee hours, and then running an increasingly substantial and complex organization during office hours.

There was no possibility of going back to sleep by the time I stopped working at about 7:30 a.m. I had to shift gears, head for the office, and get busy with Blue Metropolis programming, fundraising, and administrative responsibilities. My day rarely finished before 6:30 or 7 p.m.

It's no wonder that I thought about what a pleasure it would be to spend my life just reading and writing. I spent years longing to be the kind of writer who had the luxury of devoting herself entirely to her work. I'd done that, often enough, on weekends and on holiday mornings—getting up and going straight to the computer, sipping coffee, writing till I dropped. I always had high hopes, on those mornings, imagining I'd get many hours of work done, but it never turned out as I expected. No matter how much time stretched ahead of me, I was unable to write for more than a few hours—often the same length of time I put in on weekdays.

But those weekends did teach me something else. The longer I write, and the more emotionally charged my writing is, the more I need to go back to bed when I'm done. If I don't, I'll be able to shop, for example, or cook, or reply to a few emails, but I won't be all there. My head will still be in my book. So, the reason it was such a strain when I had to head into Blue Met is that I really needed to be back in bed.

THE WORK I always enjoyed most at Blue Metropolis was programming—reading new books, inviting authors, dreaming up events, discussing them with participants, and finding the perfect host for that particular session.

As time went on, though, I was spending less time on programming and more on fundraising, in part because I had staff who could carry out the work I enjoyed most and no one capable of bringing in the big bucks. Much of the fundraising fell to me—I wrote all the grant applications and most of the letters and proposals required by foundations and corporate donors—and to volunteers willing to open doors in the private sector.

Fundraising is inevitably competitive and demanding, and a literary festival is a priority for very few philanthropists. Health and education are the priorities, and to the extent that the arts interest donors at all, the glitziest performance arts—the opera, the symphony, the ballet—have more appeal than quiet and often cerebral literary activities.

The inherent difficulty of fundraising for the festival intensified in 2008, in the wake of the recession. Money was short, demands from all sectors increased, and donors were more reluctant than ever to donate. The volunteer support that was essential in fundraising was in short supply, too, by this time. Where once I had had to frame two or perhaps three different pitches to have any hope that one might succeed, I now had to write proposal after proposal with nary a bite.

The heady excitement of the early years had faded by this time, too. I started looking for a way out.

I planned my departure carefully, knowing this would significantly impact the organization—and keenly aware too, naturally, of the effect it would have on my own income. I wanted to leave when the organization's finances were in good shape, and there had been years when the festival ran a small deficit. We emerged in the black in 2010, which was when I made my move.

I sold my car, which I no longer needed, as I took public transit to work and could walk to the shops. My sons had all moved out, by this time, and I put my big apartment in Notre-Dame-de-Grâce on the market. When it sold, I bought myself a small apartment outright in Westmount. With my John Abbott pension kicking in, and my expenses substantially reduced, I handed in my resignation, effective at the end of December 2010.

What I wanted, when I left Blue Metropolis, was to write full time. That would be the realization of another dream.

Or so I thought.

HOW COULD I not have noticed that practically no one writes full time?

If Ella, a published novelist, spends time focusing on the work of Beatrice, another writer—writing an appreciation of Beatrice's work, say, or a biography, or including her work in course materials—is Ella working as a writer? How do you divide the writing Ella does about Beatrice's work from the writing Ella does as a novelist?

And what about Beatrice, who has herself been inspired by the novels of Doris Lessing? That is a wonderful form of appreciation. And Doris herself was inspired as a writer by the stories she heard when she was growing up in Southern Rhodesia.

How many of us, in other words, spend our lives entirely on the slopes of Mount Olympus? I have known hundreds of writers from all over the world, and I haven't met a single god. Or a single goddess, for that matter.

I did know that leaving Blue Met would be a big transition. Much as I wanted to move on, I knew I would miss the intensity of festival work.

What I was going to miss most, I decided, was the feeling of being in the swim. Though swimming itself is a solitary pursuit, there are others in the pool, so it's almost always a communal activity. Some swimmers move fast, and some with difficulty; some do their best to shoulder you out of your lane, and some make way for you. You see some of them every time you go swimming, and they look at you as though your paths have never crossed, and some of them smile. I love being in the swim.

WHAT I WOULD love most, though, was going back to bed after my morning writing.

And yes, a sleep is restorative, but that lasts how long? An hour or two, at most.

I knew from experience that writing later in the day was counterproductive. When I did go back to my computer in the afternoon or evening, I could get more writing done, but when I finally stopped, the work was still buzzing around in my brain, and I found it hard to sleep at night—and then I was unable to work the next morning, when I was fresh.

So, I knew I had to rule out the idea of a second shift. But there are twenty-four hours in every single day. Writing might take up three or four hours, sleeping eight, shopping and eating two or three. That's fifteen hours, max. What was I going to do with the rest of my day?

I WANTED TO be in the thick of it. Out and about, marvelling and enjoying. I love the excitement of the literary milieu. I often enjoy book launches and other literary parties, especially the ones I don't have to organize myself. I love talking about books I've read and writers I admire. I love being part of a merry gang of literary activists. I love getting together and talking about what's wrong and what's needed. I love working with others and changing the world.

DANY LAFERRIÈRE IS an unusual writer in numerous ways. Remarkable for the sensuousness of his work, for its playfulness, and for its seriousness, he is the only Canadian writer and the only Haitian to have been invited to become an "immortal"—a member of the Académie française.

Many writers, perhaps most, like talking about other writers and artists, but it's common for writers to view their own work and that of others as different kinds of interests. Laferrière is one of the few I know who proudly defends his interest in other writers and who feels an obligation to help a writer he likes become better known. "That's part of the literary economy, that idea," he says. "There's nothing charitable or Christian about it; it's just about spreading the word about someone you think is better than you. Helping another writer become known is even more important than writing."[36]

Laferrière's work is always personal, and his narrators are versions of himself, variously called Man, or Vieux, or Old Bones, or Laferrière,[37] but this is not autofiction. Writing so much about other writers (and about painters and musicians, as well), he says, "ensures you don't fall into narcissism."

This makes perfect sense to me. I cannot imagine writing without references and allusions to other writers, for a start. I love sharing my admiration for other writers and have gone out of my way to promote them throughout my career, by including their work in a course I was teaching, running a festival to showcase their talent, writing about them, editing them, or publishing their work. My work, like my world, is full of writers.

I HAD LOVED working on *Matrix* magazine, and when I left Blue Metropolis, I decided that, in addition to writing, I would become a publisher.

I set up a website in March 2011, designed the ".ll." logo I've used ever since, and started publishing online on a collective blog called *Salon .ll.* In June, I incorporated Linda Leith Éditions—which was from the start also known as Linda Leith Publishing—and announced the publication of our first books, which were launched at the fourteenth Blue Metropolis Festival in April 2012.

THE END OF my Blue Metropolis career was a time of momentous change in my personal life, as well. How this happened should get a book of its own, but it has to be touched on here.

The short version is that, a few months before I left Blue Met, a friend introduced me to a retired gentleman named David Gawley, who had been widowed earlier in 2010. I had been on my own for more than fifteen years by this time, and was doing well in my life as a single woman. I wasn't looking for the good man who is famously hard to find, and it might be that that's why I found him.

When David called me for the first time, he suggested he might know more about me than I did about him. He certainly did, for he had read my book *Marrying Hungary*. There being no better way to a writer's heart than to read her book, he was off to a good start.

When we met for lunch a week later, he was interested in hearing more about my summers at the Manoir Richelieu. His own summer job, when he was a student at the University of Toronto, had been as a tour guide on the steamships that used to travel from Lake Ontario to Murray Bay and up the Saguenay. I liked his intelligent blue eyes and found him kind and modest.

Surprisingly political, too. I had assumed, from his short hair, his slightly rumpled cotton shirts, and his corporate career at Canadian Pacific, that he was politically conservative. I learned otherwise when we first went out to dinner.

Though hardly a romantic topic, Statistics Canada became the news story of the day that fall when the Tory government scrapped the long-form census on which countless government policies and programs depended for reliable data. I had been following developments closely, but it turned out that David knew far more about the StatsCan issue than I did, and that he was even more outraged than I.

We soon found ourselves in love. The following April, he told me that his goal in life was to make me happy. I looked at him in disbelief. No one had ever said anything like that to me before, and I couldn't, for all my reading, think of a single romantic hero who would have expressed such a wish.

I thought we should live apart and see each other often for dinners and weekends, concerts and travel. He eventually persuaded me there were good reasons we should marry.

And then, one day in May 2012, he fell and broke his arm. He couldn't even open a bottle of wine, so I just had to move in with him.

One reason our story has to be touched on in a book about my literary life is that David has also become my partner and co-conspirator in publishing, and I doubt I could have kept the company going in these difficult times without his business experience, his acumen, and his wisdom.

We were married in September 2012, and he has taught me what marriage can be. It has to do with trust. Life has taught us both to need that.

David and I live together in intimacy and harmony, making each other happier than either of us had imagined possible.

Like a Cat

I have told the story of my first marriage in *Marrying Hungary* and the story of how the festival came to be in *Writing in the Time of Nationalism*. Writing today, in 2020, ten years after I moved on from Blue Metropolis, I have tried not to go over material I wrote about in those books. Impossible as it has been to succeed entirely in this, this is a very different book. My story looks different to me today than it did ten or fifteen years ago, for a start. And mine isn't one story, anyway. How could it be, when I've led so many different lives? Like a cat.

One life after another, some lasting two years, some three, some ten or twenty or more, a whole succession of overlapping, different lives. Except that there were gaps, too, unsettled periods between what had been and what was about to be. Which is when I accidentally rediscovered an earlier moment.

"We are not merely more weary because of yesterday," the young Beckett wrote in *Proust*—his MA thesis for

Trinity College Dublin—"we are other, no longer what we were before the calamity of yesterday."[38]

Sometimes, in some ways, yesterday was a calamity. One calamity after another. I can't say I feel weary, though; energetic is a better word for me, at least until I drop. And I am undoubtedly "other," in the sense that Beckett uses the word. Each life I've led is so different from all the others, in different countries, in different circumstances, but always—even on return visits to Northern Ireland—among foreigners. Different linguistically, too, in languages understood and spoken, badly spoken, unspoken, broken, and all but forgotten.

So different, in fact, and so packed with emotion that it's no wonder I sometimes forget what really happened. The miracle is that so much of it does come back, just as the work of Samuel Beckett—to which I gave little thought in the decades after 1975—has come back to me while working on this new book.

Harriet Armstrong has come back to me, too. She's the woman I met at St. MacNissi's College in County Antrim, whose mother remembered my father as a gentle doctor in 1949. Telling me this, Harriet threw confusion into my view of my father, forcing me to reconsider what kind of person he was—and to realize there was something I didn't know about what had happened to him after we left Lisburn.

Desmond never talked about what had happened. It wasn't until the turn of this century that Nan told me about the crisis they had lived through in the early 1950s, and about Desmond's history of mental illness.

Not having understood why Daddy and I were so often at odds, I puzzled over what Harriet had said until Nan filled in the missing piece of the puzzle.

Nan was happy I was taking notes and writing her stories down. And it was as I was writing that I found myself thinking about Desmond not only in outrage, as in the distant past, and not only in bewilderment, as in later years, but in sorrow.

WRITING DOES THAT. Wherever you start, the writing leads you down a certain path, and as you turn a corner, you can see what you left behind, some of it apparently trivial, some of it less trivial—and all of it now so vivid that you can't imagine how it could ever have slipped your mind.

You loop back, retrace your steps, sure you've taken the wrong turn. You get lost, you press on, you despair, you take heart, and eventually you end up right back where you started, if that really is where you started.

And when you're finally able to see what you've left behind, it isn't only the past that is illuminated; the present is, too. Not the future, of course not—except to the extent that the past and the present can prepare you for whatever comes next.

WRITING THIS BOOK has opened a window into several of these different selves. A toddler instructed on the National Health Service in rural Northern Ireland. A little girl nibbling sorrel in a corner of a vast garden. A seven-year-old in Basel studying a tranquillizer ad in a glossy magazine. An adolescent on a beach in County Sligo. A McGill student inspired by *Adolphe*. A young woman longing to escape a domineering father. A Canadian mother becoming a writer in Budapest. An anglophone creating a multilingual literary festival in Montreal. An older woman taking notes from her own mother. Other selves—each one different from every other—at other times, in other places.

Much of what I've discovered in the process of writing is material I had entirely forgotten until I started writing. That is as true today as it was in the early 1990s, when writing about the books I read as a child reawakened long-suppressed memories of Basel. When I start writing, I have no way of knowing where I will end up, on the last page. No way of knowing there could be any connection between the forbidden pleasures of sorrel leaves and a bowl of soup I enjoyed beside the Danube.

THIS BOOK IS an exploration, an essay—an attempt at saying what I don't yet know, what I don't know any more, and what I had no way of knowing. A reminder of much I've left behind. A glimpse at what I have become. A prelude to whatever comes next.

It takes the form of a story. There was no other way of making those discoveries than by writing and rewriting—and then rewriting some more, it seems interminable—until the story I'm telling eventually makes sense of what never did make sense.

This is what writing can do.

6.
Afterword

Afterword

My memory is unreliable, like most people's memories. That did not stop me thinking, once upon a time, that it was possible for me to write a memoir, which was cheeky of me.

Marrying Hungary, which is the title of the memoir, is as true as I could make it. Which is not the same thing as saying that it's true. Some of it is true, and some is not. There are a few reasons for this.

My memory failed me, for a start. I was protecting people, too; this is not something I recommend, but it's hard to avoid when so many of the people you're writing about are people you love. The main reason that so much of it isn't true is that I didn't tell the whole story. I couldn't. Some pieces of the puzzle were simply missing.

Memoir invites questions about me, my life, my parents, my family, the men I married, the friends who have mattered to me. Some of those are good subjects, but they're not subjects that a reader can check up on. As a reader, you won't know much more about most of these subjects than you'll find in my books, which is why it's the books that matter. The words on the page. When asked, Samuel Beckett said he knew nothing more about Godot than you'll find in the play.

The questions you might want me to answer may be intelligent and thoughtful, but if they're addressed to me, they're addressed to the wrong person. The woman who has written my books is not the woman to whom you are addressing your questions. My life was a mystery to me, and it's hardly been an open book to others. My parents are no longer alive. Close as my brothers and sisters are to me in many ways, they live far away and have led very different lives from my own.

I'm in all my books. And how could I not be? There I am, in the corners of my first book, on Hugh MacLennan's *Two Solitudes*. I may seem to be more present in *Birds of Passage*, more so in *Marrying Hungary*, but then I'm always present, in everything I've written, in whatever genre.

This doesn't mean that what happens to the fictional characters I write about has happened to me. It doesn't work like that. It doesn't mean I am any of those characters. There are similarities, but you have no way of knowing what those are, exactly. I myself am unsure about that. Something I thought obvious in one book turns out in the next one to have been misleading or insufficient or wrong. It's hard to see me. I'm somewhere over there, in the shadows, making things up. Revealing so much and no more, discovering so much and no more, in a lifelong game of hide-and-seek.

The book you've been reading features so many different versions of me that I seldom recognize myself. I catch glimpses of a girl and then a woman who is a stranger to me, like a friend I lost touch with long ago.

6. Afterword

Occasionally, I'll glimpse a character who looks familiar enough, like someone I think I know, but then she turns around and does something I would never do, like marry.

The question I've been wrestling with over the past few years is how to turn all this into a narrative. I've wrestled with this question because I haven't really wished to know the answer, but I do somehow have to find a way of creating that narrative.

If I knew the answer, I might never write again. Much of what you have read in these pages explores what I discovered as I was writing. The whole point is that writing is a process of discovery, of becoming, and of change. The change is in me. Someone new emerges whenever I break the silence, and the woman who picks up the finished book is necessarily a different woman than the one who started it. I'm the one who's hiding, despite all my efforts, and I'll always be the one who's seeking.

Besides, I'm wiser now, and I know better than to call this book—any book—a memoir. Every time I check something, I see I got something wrong, that I always got something wrong. I get dates wrong and misspell the name of a school I went to for three years. I change people's names and mix up what happened when and who said what to whom. I don't mean to be difficult. I'm doing my best, fixing everything I can, in the interests of truth and in the interests of the story. I know for sure it's not all true. Better not to pretend otherwise.

So, I think of this as an essay: an attempt at approximating what really happened. A prose work, certainly. It has an uncertain basis in what really happened to someone who resembles the girl, the adolescent, the young woman, the older woman—all the characters I might have been, once upon a time.

Notes

1   William Allingham, "The Fairies," in *Sixteen Poems by William Allingham: Selected by William Butler Yeats* (Dundrum, Ireland: The Dun Emer Press, 2005), http://www.gutenberg.org/files/16839/16839-h/16839-h.htm#THE_FAIRIES.

2   In the wake of Toni Morrison's death in 2019, I was interested in much that I learned about her, including this comment: "If you find a book you really want to read but it hasn't been written yet, then you must write it." (From Ellen Brown, "Writing Is Third Career for Morrison," *The Cincinnati Enquirer*, September 27, 1981, F-11.)

3   George Bernard Shaw, *Pygmalion* (Harmondsworth, Middlesex: Penguin Classics, 2003), 8.

4   Zadie Smith, "Speaking in Tongues," in *Changing My Mind: Occasional Essays* (New York: Hamish Hamilton, 2009), 133.

5   A.J. Cronin, *The Citadel* (London: Victor Gollancz Ltd., 1937).

6   Nancy Mitford, ed., *Noblesse Oblige* (Harmondsworth, Middlesex: Penguin Books, 1959). Mitford's essay is "The English Aristocracy," 35–56.

261

7   Alan S.C. Ross, "U and Non-U: An Essay in Sociological Linguistics," in Mitford, *Noblesse Oblige*, 9–32.

8   Alice Gregory, "Lessons from the Last Swiss Finishing School," *The New Yorker*, October 8, 2018, https://www.newyorker.com/magazine/2018/10/08/lessons-from-the-last-swiss-finishing-school.

9   Mitford, "The English Aristocracy," 38–39.

10   Gully Wells, *The House in France* (New York: Knopf, 2011).

11   Thomas Moore, *A Selection of Irish Melodies* (London: William Power, 1908), 133, https://archive.org/details/MooreIrishMelodies17/page/n97/mode/2up?q=Believe+me.

12   Wisława Szymborska, "Three Oddest Words," in *Poems New and Collected*, trans. Stanislaw Baránczak and Clare Cavanagh (New York: Harcourt, 1998), 261.

13   Paul Delbouille's critical edition of *Adolphe* (Paris: Les Belles lettres, 1977), 3:121, is the basis for this translation, edited by Patrick Coleman, trans. Margaret Mauldon (New York: Oxford University Press, 2001), 15–16.

14   Germaine de Staël-Holstein, *Corinne, ou l'Italie*, https://gallica.bnf.fr/ark:/12148/bpt6k6125704m/f438.image.

15   Renee Winegarten, *Germaine de Staël and Benjamin Constant: A Dual Biography* (New Haven: Yale University Press, 2008), 1.

16   Mary Beard, *Women & Power: A Manifesto* (New York: Liveright, 2017), 81.

17   Jenny Turner, "Dame Muriel Spark," *Guardian*, April 17, 2006, https://www.theguardian.com/news/2006/apr/17/guardianobituaries.booksobituaries.

18   Muriel Spark, *Curriculum Vitae: A Volume of Autobiography* (London: Houghton Mifflin, 1992).

19 Highly accomplished autobiographical works by men include Martin Amis's *Experience: A Memoir* (New York: Vintage, 2001); Will Aitken's *Antigone Undone* (Regina: University of Regina Press, 2018), and Mark Abley's *The Organist* (Regina: University of Regina Press, 2019).

20 Beard, 28.

21 Mavis Gallant, interview with Linda Leith, quoted in *Writing in the Time of Nationalism* (Winnipeg: Signature, 2010), 32.

22 Linda Leith, ed., *Telling Differences: New English Fiction from Quebec* (Montreal: Véhicule Press, 1988).

23 Linda Leith, *Introducing Hugh MacLennan's Two Solitudes* (Toronto: ECW Press, 1990).

24 Toni Morrison, as quoted in Hilton Als, "Ghosts in the House: How Toni Morrison Fostered a Generation of Black Writers," *The New Yorker,* October 27, 2003, reprinted in the July 27, 2020 issue, 32.

25 Gallant, interview with Linda Leith, 32.

26 Edna Longley, *From Cathleen to Anorexia: The Breakdown of Irelands* [LIP Pamphlet] (Dublin: Attic Press,1990).

27 A.J. Cronin, *Country Doctor* (London: Victor Gollancz Ltd., 1935).

28 Smith, 134.

29 Pauline Kael, "The Man from Dream City," *The New Yorker*, July 14, 1975, https://www.newyorker.com/magazine/1975/07/14/the-man-from-dream-city.

30 Dany Laferrière, *The Return*, trans. David Homel (Vancouver: Douglas & McIntyre, 2009), 44.

31 Samuel Beckett, *Proust* (London: Chatto & Windus, 1930), 31.

32 It was later renamed Festival international de la littérature.

33   Smith, 134.

34   Willliam H. Gass, *On Being Blue: A Philosophical Enquiry* (New York: D.R. Godine, 1975).

35   Louis Gauthier, *Voyage en Irlande avec un parapluie* (Montreal: Éditions de l'Homme, 1994). Translated into English by Linda Leith as *Travels with an Umbrella: An Irish Journey* (Winnipeg: Signature Editions, 2000).

36   From Adam Leith Gollner, *Working in a Bathtub: Conversations with the Immortal Dany Laferrière* (Montreal: Linda Leith Publishing, 2020), 96.

37   Gollner, *Working in a Bathtub*, 6.

38   Beckett, 3.

Linda Leith Recommends

A personal selection of modern imaginative and autobiographical writing, including just one title by many of the authors mentioned in *The Girl from Dream City* and by a few other authors I recommend.

Athill, Diana. *Stet: An Editor's Life*. New York: Grove Press, 2002.

Atwood, Margaret. *Alias Grace*. New York: Doubleday, 1996.

Beckett, Samuel. *Murphy*. London: Routledge, 1938.

Blais, Marie-Claire. *Mad Shadows*. Translated by Merloyd Lawrence. Toronto: New Canadian Library, 1971.

Bowen, Elizabeth. *The Heat of the Day*. London: Knopf, 1948.

Charney, Ann. *Dobryd*. Toronto: New Press, 1973.

Conway, Jill Ker. *The Road from Coorain*. New York: Vintage, 1990.

Cusk, Rachel. *Outline*. New York: Farrar, Straus & Giroux, 2015.

Drabble, Margaret. *The Middle Ground*. London: Knopf, 1980.

Forster, E.M. *Howards End*. London: Edward Arnold, 1910.

Gallant, Mavis. *From the Fifteenth District*. New York: Random House, 1979.

Gibb, Camilla. *This Is Happy: A Memoir*. Toronto: Doubleday Canada, 2015.

Gildiner, Catherine. *Too Close to the Falls: A Memoir*. Toronto: ECW Press, 2005.

Hazzard, Shirley. *The Great Fire*. New York: Farrar, Straus & Giroux, 2003.

Ishiguro, Kazuo. *An Artist of the Floating World*. London: Faber & Faber, 1986.

Joyce, James. *Portrait of the Artist as a Young Man*. New York: B.W. Huebsch, 1916.

Kellough, Kaie. *Accordéon*. Winnipeg: ARP Books, 2017.

Koval, Ramona. *By the Book: A Reader's Guide to Life*. Melbourne: Text Publishing, 2012.

Ladoo, Harold Sonny. *No Pain Like This Body*. Toronto: House of Anansi Press, 1972.

Laferrière, Dany. *How To Make Love to a Negro Without Getting Tired*. Translated by David Homel. Vancouver: Douglas & McIntyre, 1985.

Lawrence, D.H. *Sons and Lovers*. London: Duckworth, 1913.

LeGuin, Ursula K. *The Left Hand of Darkness*. New York: Ace Books, 1969.

Lessing, Doris. *Martha Quest*. London: Michael Joseph Ltd., 1952.

Macdonald, Helen. *H Is for Hawk*. New York: Grove Press, 2016.

Mansfield, Katherine. *Bliss and Other Stories*. New York: Knopf, 1920.

Marsh, Ngaio. *Surfeit of Lampreys*. London: Collins Crime Club, 1941.

Moore, Brian. *The Lonely Passion of Judith Hearne*. London: André Deutsch, 1955.

Morrison, Toni. *Sula*. New York: Knopf, 1973.

Mukherjee, Bharati. *The Tiger's Daughter*. New York: Houghton Mifflin, 1971.

Munro, Alice. *Lives of Girls and Women*. Toronto: McGraw-Hill Ryerson, 1971.

Nabokov, Vladimir. *Speak, Memory: An Autobiography Revisited*. London: Victor Gollancz, 1951.

Nafisi, Azar. *Reading Lolita in Tehran: A Memoir in Books*. New York: Random House, 2003.

Ondaatje, Michael. *In the Skin of a Lion*. Toronto: McClelland & Stewart, 1987.

Rhys, Jean. *Wide Sargasso Sea*. London: André Deutsch, 1966.

Roy, Gabrielle. *The Tin Flute*. Translated by Hannah Josephson. New York: Reynal and Hitchcock, 1947.

Sarsfield, Mairuth. *No Crystal Stair*. Toronto: Stoddart, 1998.

Sayers, Dorothy L. *Strong Poison*. London: Victor Gollancz, 1930.

Smith, Zadie. *On Beauty*. New York: Hamish Hamilton, 2005.

Sontag, Susan. *Illness as Metaphor*. New York: Farrar, Straus & Giroux, 1978.

Spark, Muriel. *Loitering with Intent*. London: Bodley Head, 1981.

Szabó, Magda. *The Door*. Translated by Len Rix. New York: New York Review Books Classics, 2015.

Thuy, Kim. *Ru*. Translated by Sheila Fischman. Toronto: Vintage Canada, 2012.

Woolf, Virginia. *Orlando: A Biography*. London: Hogarth Press, 1928.

Acknowledgements

I am eternally grateful to the writers who have inspired me and especially to Mavis Gallant, who became a friend. A vital role has also been played by the writers, translators, publishers, and readers who belong to the literary milieu I am part of, which never fails to challenge and sustain me. This is a world I love, and one in which I have thrived. Most of it is located near where I live in Montreal, some in other parts of Canada, and some across the globe.

I wish to acknowledge a great debt to Adam Leith Gollner, David Gawley, Ann Charney, Patrick Coleman, and Leila Marshy for taking the time to read and comment on different versions of this book. All remaining errors and omissions are my own.

My thanks to Bruce Walsh and his successor as director of the University of Regina Press, Kristine Luecker, as well as to Kelly Laycock, David McLennan, Kendra Ward, and other members of the team in Regina.

My appreciation and gratitude to Marianne Ackerman, David Caron, Jan Curtis, Simon Dardick and Nancy Marelli, Jack David, Louise Dupré, András B. Göllner, Melanie Grondin, Katia Grubisic, Karen Haughian, Annie Heminway, Susan Henderson, Mikhail Iossel, Jean-Marie Jot, Zsuzsa Körösi and Michel Emsalem, Julie Keith, Ramona Koval, Phyllis Lambert, Marie-Andrée Lamontagne, Anna Leventhal, Yan Liang, Mary K. MacLeod, Elizabeth McIninch, Elise Moser, Margaret O'Brien, Ève Pariseau, Shelley Pomerance, Robin Porter, Kenneth Radu and Diane Hibbard, Judit Rajk and the late László Rajk, William St. Hilaire, Lori Schubert, Peter Scowen, Linda Tracey, André Vanasse, Patterson Webster, and the many other friends, colleagues, and co-conspirators who have enriched my life.

I would like to single out the late Patrick Baker for special thanks. When I was an unhappy teenager who aspired to write, he spent the time to encourage my reading and my writing. We did lose touch, eventually, but he wrote to me, late in his life, to let me know how he had been following my career and how proud he was of me. I wrote back at once, asking to see him, but he chose not to respond, and I was saddened to learn he died soon afterwards.

My love to Ian, Brian, Sheelagh, and Mandy Jo Leith, and to Tesni Daniel, William Taylor, and Mandy Leith. To Adam, Michael, and Julian Gollner, Annie Briard, to Laura L. Taylor, Sam Taylor, James Gittings, and George Leith, and to my grandson Remy Kaslo Briard Gollner, the first of a new generation.

I dedicate this book to my darling Granny Jo and my matchless parents, Nan and Desmond.

Linda Leith

PHOTO: COURTESY LINDA LEITH

ABOUT THE AUTHOR

Born in Northern Ireland, LINDA LEITH attended schools in Belfast, London, Basel, Paris, and Montreal, graduating from the University of London, which granted her a PhD on the work of Samuel Beckett when she was twenty-six. A novelist, essayist, literary translator, and the founder of Blue Metropolis International Literary Festival and of Linda Leith Publishing, Leith was named an Officer of the Order of Canada in 2020. She lives in Montreal.

THE REGINA COLLECTION

Named as a tribute to Saskatchewan's capital city with
its rich history of boundary-defying innovation, The
Regina Collection builds upon University of Regina
Press's motto of "a voice for many peoples." Intimate
in size and beautifully packaged, these books aim to
tell the stories of those who have been caught up in
social and political circumstances beyond their control.

To see other books in *The Regina Collection*, visit
WWW.UOFRPRESS.CA